UNBELIEVABLE CRIMES VOLUME THREE: MACABRE YET
UNKNOWN TRUE CRIME STORIES

First edition. May 22, 2023.

Written by Daniela Airlie.

Table of Contents

Prologue

As we embark on the third volume of the *Unbelievable Crimes* series, we are confronted with the dark underbelly of society that a lot of individuals often prefer to ignore. The crimes explored in this book are undeniably unpleasant, but I believe they are important to document and remember. These are the stories of lives brutally snuffed out and of the families left shattered by the evil actions of the depraved. We know about the big-headline crimes, but what about the similarly despicable crimes that slip through the cracks of the media?

If you're new to the series, let me introduce you to the premise. *Unbelievable Crimes* explores the stories that are often overlooked by mainstream media, becoming mere statistics in the grand scheme of true crime data. But their stories deserve to be told and the victims' voices deserve to be heard.

The series tackles hard-to-hear cases that may leave you feeling disturbed: crimes of "passion", of greed, of revenge. Horrific crimes against children. Acts of depraved torture, malice, and sickening abuse. Crimes that were carried out by purportedly ordinary people, living seemingly ordinary lives.

It's a truly terrifying reality that the criminals discussed in this book were once regarded as decent members of society. However, it does help us come to the realization that violent criminals and killers are those that walk among us: people we walk past in the street, our neighbors, or even our acquaintances. If you go by the *six degrees of separation* theory, we're never more than six (or fewer) individuals away from being connected to a murderer. It's a macabre idea, but one that checks out the more you think about it.

For example, your aunt's friend may have a cousin who is behind bars for murder. Your co-worker's daughter's husband may have served time for a violent attack years ago. The person who served your coffee this morning may have a sister who was best friends with a murderer. The *six degrees* notion isn't that far-fetched if we sit and think about it. In fact, if we each delved into our family history, we may find we're even closer to horrific crimes than we'd ever imagined possible.

It's a pretty dark way to view things, I agree, but it reinforces the reality that we are surrounded by individuals like those covered in this book. Those with malicious intent and violent tendencies just waiting to be unleashed. Victims can be anybody, from anywhere, with any kind of background. As can criminals.

As well as this, it's also important to note that reading about violent crimes can be emotionally taxing. Some details in this book may be disturbing to learn about. Still, we are here to pay tribute to the victims and to ensure that their stories are not forgotten, even if they're hard to absorb. At the same time though, some of these tales will remind us of the resilience and strength of the human spirit.

With that said, if you're ready, let's begin.

We Didn't Like Her

As the saying goes, *two's company, three's a crowd*. For 16-year-old Skylar Neese, her friendship group of three was solid - until Shelia Eddy and Rachel Shoaf took a dislike to her. Instead of ending the friendship with Skylar, the pair chose to end her life instead.

It seems teen girls can act in a brutal fashion where friendships and relationships are concerned. In *Volume Two,* I covered the case of Michele Avila whose two best friends murdered her over their shared jealousy of her. In *Volume One,* I recounted the case of Lorraine Thorpe, a teen girl who helped kill a vulnerable woman for no reason at all. In a shocking twist, she then went on to aid in the murder of her father just days after this, alongside her older role model and alleged boyfriend, Paul Clarke.

Then there's the case of Payton Leutner, whose 12-year-old friends lured her to the woods with the purpose of stabbing her to death. Thankfully, she survived, but the intent was still there from her school friends: the young girls wanted to kill in a brutal fashion. The story I'm about to cover is similarly savage and senseless.

Skylar Annette Neese was your typical adolescent. Like most 16-year-olds, she spent much of her time with her friends or on social media. She would regularly post updates about her life and was often open when sharing her personal life online. If she had an argument with her friends, the drama would find itself online, as is often the case with teens who are dealing with newfound emotions such as heartbreak and feelings of loneliness. As well as her social media addiction, Skylar spent her time outside of school working at a local fast-food joint in her hometown of Star City, West Virginia. She enjoyed having a job, the independence, and the extra money it brought in, so she never missed a shift.

Her two best friends were Shelia Eddy and Rachel Shoaf. Skylar had known Sheila for almost a decade, and the duo met Rachel in freshman year. The group was fast friends, going everywhere together and confiding in one another about their worries or anxieties. While the gang was undeniably close, there was a noticeable difference between Skylar and her two best friends. Sheila and Rachel's parents had divorced, while Skylar's mother and father were still together. Skylar's home life was stable, calm, and an environment of nourishment for the teen. This created an unseen divide between the trio, with Skylar unknowingly segregated from her two friends as time went by.

Skylar's mother would later say she felt her daughter tried to keep Sheila on the straight and narrow, explaining how her daughter's friend was wild and reckless in her decision-making. Still, Mary Neese would invite Sheila into the family fold, so much so that the girl would simply walk into the Neese's house without knocking and make herself at home. She was a part of the family, Mary would say, and a ball of fun and lightheartedness.

Rachel Shoaf was the quieter member of the group, but she seemingly looked up to Sheila and her breezy outlook on life. Rachel had a more strict home life, with her family imposing tighter curfews and rules than those of her peers' parents. The same could be said for Skylar too, who would be given less freedom than the loudest member of the group, Sheila. The differences between the girls would cause teenage spats, which were often played out online. In the spring of 2012, Skylar posted an indirect status on social media, calling an unnamed friend a "two-faced bitch." She would also refer to the unspecified person as "stupid" and would later call out her two friends by writing "too bad my friends are having lives without me." The tight-knit trio was quickly crumbling for all to see.

The teenage turmoil soon became subtle bullying. The girls' peers picked up on Skylar becoming pushed out of the group, with one incident playing out in front of an entire class, when a phone call of Sheila and Skylar fighting was put on loudspeaker by Rachel. Skylar had no idea anyone other than Sheila was on the call, let alone a whole group of people she knew.

Skylar spent that summer taking as many shifts at work as she could. Her friends were proving unreliable, and work was a distraction. When Skylar didn't turn up for her designated shift on July 7, 2012, there was an immediate cause for concern. The girl had never called in sick, let alone just not showed up for work. Sadly, the worry was warranted.

Around the same time that Skylar's coworkers were trying to contact the teen, her family was scrambling to find out where she was, too. Her bedroom window was wide open, but she hadn't taken off with any of her belongings. A well-known phone addict, Skylar had left her charger at home. She'd also left behind essentials such as clothing, a toothbrush, or any cash. Skylar was a typical teen, but she'd never ran away before. She'd never had any reason to; although her parents were on the stricter side, they gave her plenty of freedom and time to socialize. Police were quickly called.

The Neese family were beside themselves. Hours dragged by, and no word from either Skylar or the police. Eventually, the phone rang. It was Sheila. It offered Mary Neese some comfort that Sheila was able to give more to the story as to where Skylar may have gone. Apparently, along with Rachel Shoaf, the trio spent the night prior driving around smoking weed, and gossiping. The girls had picked Skylar up and dropped her off away from the Neese house so they didn't get their friend in trouble for sneaking out. According to Sheila, though, they'd dropped Skylar not too far from her house. It seemed something - or someone - must have got in the way of her reaching home.

This notion was bought for a little while. After all, the teens had admitted to smoking weed in their story. Surely if they knew anything more than they were letting on, they wouldn't implicate themselves by admitting to taking drugs the night Skylar went missing?

However, the two girls couldn't help but make themselves look guilty when their stories didn't add up.

Sheila said they'd picked Skylar up at 11 pm. The Neese household had a CCTV camera that captured the road right outside their property, a fact Sheila may not have known. An inspection of the footage from the night Skylar vanished showed it was 12:30 am before the girls turned up for her, not 11 pm as Sheila had said. Rachel wasn't around to speak to since she'd headed off to summer camp after Skylar's disappearance. Sheila didn't just get the time wrong by ten or fifteen minutes, or even by half an hour. It seemed she'd misinformed the police on purpose.

The police investigation led them to speak to Skylar's classmates and friends, many of whom repeated the same story: the last they'd heard, Skylar had gone to a party the night she vanished, and took a fatal dose of heroin. Apparently, the partygoers in attendance panicked at the sight of the teen's dead body and made a pact to dispose of Skylar themselves. No names were mentioned, of course, which led police to become suspicious. Surely if something so horrific had happened, these kids would know the name of the people who buried the teenager's body?

The police's intuition kept bringing them back to Shelia Eddy and Rachel Shoaf. They noticed Shiela wasn't acting "normal"; as normal as you can be when your best friend has vanished, anyway. Her behavior felt off to the officers looking into Skylar's disappearance. When they caught up with Rachel, they found her to be behaving strangely, too. She was incredibly nervous, but her story echoed that of Sheila's. So much so, it seemed rehearsed.

Being nervous and acting "off" aren't reasons for arrest, however, and the investigation seemed to stall. With a suspicious eye on Sheila and Rachel, the police delved into Skylar's personal life to see if that could lead them to her. When they checked the teen's social media accounts, they found she was full of teen angst in the days leading up to her disappearance. She would post about how she was sick and tired of being at home on her own, berating her friends for hanging out without her. She also posted about being unable to trust her friends the day prior to her vanishing. While Skylar never mentioned these untrustworthy friends by name, it seemed clear she was talking about Sheila and Rachel. Again, pushing someone out of your social circle isn't cause for arrest, but police were honing in on the two girls, convinced they had something to do with the teenager's sudden disappearance.

With the girls remaining tight-lipped, authorities needed to be clever. How could they coax more information out of the friends? They had to think like teenagers. So, they monitored the girls' social media under the fake profile of a teenage boy. The girls exposed themselves as being uncaring about their best friend vanishing, and even posted pictures of just the two of them together, smiling happily. Sheila even posted a status that seemed cold, considering the circumstances. "No one on this earth can handle me and Rachel," she said. Chillingly, she added, "If you think you can, you're wrong." Police were confident that one of the girls would slip up and post something incriminating, but Rachel became much quieter on social media. Still, they were monitoring Sheila.

As the case began to receive more speculation online, the girls were receiving messages from people who were following the disappearance. They outright blamed them for killing Skylar. Understandably, this made the teenagers nervous. Messages sent their way warned them that justice was coming. Strangers commented on their social media pages to outright call them murderers. Throughout the investigation, both girls were brought in for additional questioning now and then, but their initial story was one they kept repeating.

While police waited for one of the girls to post something incriminating, perhaps if they had a falling out, they began to review CCTV of the areas Sheila Eddy's car might have been the night of the disappearance. In their trailing of her car, it led them to view CCTV from businesses in West Virginia. Sheila's car was captured driving past a store in the town of Blackstone. This meant the girls had lied to the police: they told them they'd gone east that night. They'd already got the time they'd picked Skylar up incorrect. Now they'd got their location that night completely wrong, too, by a lot. When Rachel, who was pinpointed as the weak link, was confronted with the lies she'd told, she folded - somewhat.

Her story changed to say that Skylar got out of the car and ran into the woods alone. They had no idea where she went and couldn't find her. When Sheila got wind that Rachel's version of events had shifted, she quickly changed her story to match, too. Not quite enough to count as incriminating evidence, though, so no arrests were made. Still, the girls were bound to feel the pressure since the police were circling them incessantly.

One of them would crack, they were sure.

On December 28, 2012, Patricia Shoaf made a desperate call to the police. She pleaded with the call handler to come get her daughter, Rachel. Apparently, the 16-year-old was screaming at her and hitting her. Officers attended the Shoaf residence and restrained Rachel, who'd been threatening to take her own life before she was admitted to a psychiatric unit. A few days later, on January 3, 2013, investigators headed to Chestnut Ridge, the hospital where Rachel was recovering.

They didn't need to probe her much. She confessed the truth almost as soon as officers set foot in her room. "We stabbed her," Rachel confessed tearily.

The trio had picked Skylar up in the early hours, as CCTV had shown. They drove her to a remote area, got out of the car with her, pulled out their concealed knives, and began stabbing Skylar on the count of three. They relentlessly lashed out at the defenseless girl, raining blow after blow on her until she fell to the floor. At one point, she managed to get herself up and break free from the onslaught, but the callous girls caught up with her and pierced the blade in Skylar's knee so she couldn't run away.

"Why?" Skylar cried out as her "best friends" attacked her without remorse. This would be the girl's final word.

Once the pair were satisfied that Skylar was dead, they buried her in a shallow grave topped with twigs and branches.

The murder wasn't a spontaneous act, Rachel would admit. They'd been planning it for months: Sheila would provide the murder weapons, and Rachel would get the shovel to bury the body. They arranged what cleaning materials they'd need to clear the murder scene of their DNA, and made sure to agree on a change of clothes for the aftermath. The pair agreed to begin their frenzied knife attack on the count of three to make sure they initiated it at the same time. They spent their classes plotting the murder and agreed they'd do it right before Rachel was due to attend summer camp. The date was set. They just needed to lure Skylar into the car. What better way than to suggest an evening of driving around aimlessly, having fun, and smoking weed?

Now that the police had a more honest overview of what happened to Skylar Neese, they needed to know why Rachel had felt she needed to murder her former friend. After a brief pause, she answered nonchalantly, "We didn't like her."

While this took officers aback, they still had more questions. *Where is Skylar now?* Rachel was immediately placed in a squad car, along with her attorney, and guided officers to the remote woods where she'd left Skylar's body. The girls had carried the murder out in July when the weather was scorching. It was now the beginning of January, and the thick snow skewed Rachel's ability to accurately tell the police where the body lay. Investigators had to postpone the search for Skylar's grave until the heavy snow melted, which came in mid-January. Rachel's story checked out. They found a body pierced with dozens of stab wounds under a thin layer of sticks. However, the harsh weather and decomposition of the body rendered the corpse unidentifiable. DNA testing had to be carried out, and this meant the case dragged on until March of that year.

Finally, the body was confirmed to be that of Skylar Neese, and the community of Star City was devastated. That day, Sheila, a constant on social media, posted a dedication to her late friend. "I miss you more than you'll ever know," she wrote. "You'll ALWAYS be my best friend."

Just a few weeks after the announcement of Skylar's body being found, Sheila wrote another social media status, and knowing what we know now, it's truly chilling. "We really did go on three," she said, presumably referring to the agreement she had with Rachel to begin stabbing Skylar on the count of three.

While this was going on, investigators needed more to tie Sheila to the crime than just Rachel's word. They began seizing Sheila's items, including her phone and car, where they found Skylar's blood in the trunk. Police now had enough to move in and arrest the teen, which they did on May 1, 2013, while Sheila and her mother were having lunch together at a restaurant. There was no wiggle room for Sheila to lie her way out of this, and so she had to admit culpability in the face of the evidence stacked against her. Rachel had secured a plea deal with authorities to testify against her friend in return for a lighter sentence.

Rachel pleaded guilty to second-degree murder. She was handed 30 years behind bars, with the possibility of parole after serving 10 years. While her punishment was read out, she sobbed into a handkerchief. Sheila was given life in prison with parole being a possibility after 15 years. As she was led away, she was in a zombie-like state, perhaps never expecting her wicked deed to lead to this.

Skylar's father was understandably upset with the apparent leniency his daughter's killers received. "They're both sickos," he said, adding that they're a pair of animals who deserve to be locked away forever. David Neese also said he felt he'd never get closure after his daughter's untimely end, saying "My little girl is something you can't close."

Perhaps the Neese's lack of closure is amplified by the fact they don't truly know why their child was killed. "We didn't like her," was the reason given for Skylar's brutal death, but that's a ludicrous explanation. Still to this day, it's the only explanation given. However, there have been unsubstantiated claims that Sheila and Rachel were romantically involved, and killed Skylar when she found out, fearing that she would out their secret relationship. Skylar's mother rebuffs this idea, pointing toward the fact that Skylar had lots of gay friends and wouldn't have cared if her friends had got together. Still, we know there must be *some* deeper reason they wanted to end Skylar's life; simply "not liking" her just doesn't cut it.

In a speck of light emanating from an undeniably dark situation, Skylar's murder triggered the passing of "Skylar's Law." Skylar's disappearance didn't set off an Amber Alert when police were alerted about her sudden disappearance. This is because her case didn't meet all of the criteria required by law for one to be issued. In particular, because Skylar got into Sheila's car willingly the morning she left her house, she was not considered "abducted." This was a bit of a gray area, considering it was later discovered that she'd been lured into the car under false pretenses, and therefore had been abducted. As such, Skylar's Law was passed to modify the criteria for an amber alert to be issued, making it less stringent. West Virginia would now issue an Amber Alert in any missing child case, even if the child hasn't been abducted.

As for the killers, they're both locked up at Lakin Correctional Center in West Virginia.

Rachel has reportedly married a fellow inmate, who has since been released. Rachel was eligible for parole in the spring of 2023, which was denied. Sheila is eligible for parole in 2028. David Neese vowed at their initial trial to attend every parole hearing his daughter's killers had.

Such an incredibly sad tale that's all the more tragic because there is no way to make sense of it. Even now, a decade after the crime, we're no closer to finding out why Skylar had to die. We may never know why her killers felt the urge to brutalize their former friend, which must be a painful burden for the Neese family to bear. Still, there's time for Sheila or Rachel to come forward with more details about that fateful July morning and explain why they did the awful things they did.

Five Wicked Fiends

When digesting true crime, we often have a case that hits us as being so utterly vile we have to place the book down or hit pause on the TV show we're watching. I mentioned in *Volume One* that the case of Junko Furuta troubled me for some time after learning about it. If you don't know much about it, I don't suggest learning about it unless you're prepared to hear some truly disturbing things. The ordeal teenager Junko went through prior to her death is nothing short of hell on earth, and a case that I've dedicated a lot of time to learning about, albeit in small doses. It's a case I've considered dedicating an entire book to, and I've even got the court records of the case translated from Japanese to English since there's not a great deal of widely available case data out there for this crime.

The Junko Furuta case is utterly maddening, after the initial shock of hearing the details of the crime. The case I'm about to cover evokes similar emotions. This is another case that tends to stick with you after reading it; the disturbing facts bounce around your head, trying to compute. We're left wondering, *how do we have people on this earth who are capable of such evil and violence?*

This case contains some truly disturbing information, so please bear this in mind before reading. This is a bleak tale, but one that I feel needs to be remembered, regardless.

Anita Cobby was a 26-year-old nurse with the world at her feet: she was beautiful - a beauty queen, no less - smart, and kind. Despite her beginning a potentially prosperous modeling career, her heart wasn't in it. She was a warm, considerate person whose calling was to help people. Her mother was a nurse, and Anita saw the fulfillment the career choice gave her parent, so decided to follow suit and become a registered nurse herself.

Anita was born Anita Lynch in Sydney, Australia, on November 2, 1959. A smiley, outgoing child, she made friends easily and enjoyed a stable, nurturing upbringing from her parents, Garry and Grace. As Anita entered her teens, she began partaking in beauty pageants and was crowned Miss Western Suburbs when she was 19. She enrolled in a nursing degree shortly after, and while studying toward her dream career, she met John Cobby at Sydney Hospital. There was an immediate attraction, and in March 1982, she became Mrs Cobby. The couple were in their early 20s when they tied the knot, and a few years into their union, they discovered they were completely different people compared to who they were when they first met, understandably. Some couples who marry young find they can compromise with each others differences. Others find that their differences are just too great, and divorce becomes the only option.

For Anita and John, they were working out which option they ought to choose. They loved each other, there was no doubt about it, but they were also blossoming into different individuals. They were leaning towards making it work, although they were living apart. Tragically, they'd never get the chance to smooth things out and move forward with their relationship.

On February 2, 1986, Anita finished a long shift at Sydney Hospital. After being on her feet all day, she met up with some friends for a relaxing meal and a catch-up. After finishing dinner, Anita hopped on the evening train to Blacktown, Sydney, where she was staying with her parents while on a break from living with John. The train left the station at 9.12 pm and 45 minutes later, arrived in her hometown. Tired from a long day, Anita got off the train and headed to the payphone to call her dad to collect her. This was their normal routine, especially when it was dark, as Garry didn't like his daughter walking home alone. Not that there was a great deal of crime in Blacktown, but the protective father wanted to be safe, not sorry. On that particular night, by a stroke of utter misfortune, the payphone had been vandalized to the point it was out of order. Anita had no choice but to walk home. She'd never make it there.

As she walked briskly, the orange hues of the street lamps guided her way. A white sedan pulled up alongside her, crawling beside the path she walked on. Inside the car was a group of malignant young men, five individuals you'd surely cross the street to avoid.

The car they were driving was stolen. The chief agitator was John Travers, a 19-year-old menace to society, young women, children, and animals - pretty much anything he could hurt, he would. Except perhaps a male the same age as him - that would mean a fair match. John Travers was cowardly by nature and unpleasant by look; a puny, sour-faced young man that perhaps even his mother couldn't love. She had trouble managing her wayward son, who had been violent from a young age.

He began using drugs and alcohol at age 13 and frequently carried a knife around with him. Never able to control him, his mother's health eventually deteriorated to the point Travers was placed in foster care. Again, no amount of guidance would stop Travers' mean-spiritedness, and his violence was only escalating with age.

Also in the car of reprobates was Michael Murdoch, a close friend of Travers. The pair had been friends and criminal accomplices from a young age, and Murdoch had been in juvenile detention for much of his childhood. Then there were The Murphys: three brothers with an equally abhorrent lust for violence. The eldest brother was Michael, 33, the middle brother was Gary, 28, and the youngest was Les, 22. All of them had been in trouble with the law prior to the horrific crime they were about to commit.

The group had been cruising around the dimly lit residential areas in the stolen car when they realized they were almost out of gas. None of the five had any money to pay for more, so they came to the agreement they'd rob someone off the street and fill the tank up. As they scoured the area, they happened upon Anita. The gang quickly concurred they'd steal her money. The closer they got to the woman, they changed their plan: they wouldn't just rob the woman, they'd kidnap her.

Anita glanced at the sedan rolling beside her, but before she had a chance to do anything, two of the men jumped out and bundled the terrified woman into the car. She didn't enter the vehicle quietly, though; she screamed and cried for help. Although the streets were empty and no one was about, her screams were heard by a nearby household. A young brother and sister were sitting watching TV when they heard blood-curdling shrieks coming from somewhere outside. They jumped up and ran outside, and captured the moment two men were bundling a young brunette woman into their car. "Hey! Let her go!" the teenagers yelled, to no avail. The white sedan raced off with the abductee inside. The siblings raced back inside, where their mother was calling triple zero to alert the authorities.

As the family was explaining what had gone on to the call handler, their older brother had just returned home, and as he pulled up toward the house, the siblings ran out to tell him what they'd witnessed. Still in his car, he took off to look for the culprits, searching for the white Holden his younger siblings had described. There was no doubt the woman who'd been snatched from the streets was in big trouble, and the family knew they needed to be quick if they were going to catch up with the criminals.

After a short time driving the streets, he found himself just outside Blacktown, where he scanned the area for any white vehicles that looked like a Holden. He observed a white car that was exactly as his siblings had described, parked up in an ominously remote location. He pulled up nearby, got out of the car, and headed toward the white sedan, hoping it was the right car. He had a flashlight that he used to light up the inside of the vehicle, exposing it as totally empty. With no one nearby and the car seemingly parked up for the night, it appeared it wasn't the criminal's car. After a little more scouring of the area, the concerned man had to turn back home, disappointed he wasn't able to rescue the woman.

However, the man *did* have the right car. The kidnappers were mere feet from him as he inspected it. They watched from the nearby roadside, hidden in tall foliage. The criminals observed the man until he left the scene, all the while they held Anita down forcefully, brutally clasping her mouth shut while pinning her limbs to the floor. The brave man who chased the kidnappers will no doubt have felt the painful pangs of frustration when he would later discover he was a stone's throw away from Anita Cobby that night. Tragically, a cruel twist of fate saw luck lay on the criminals' side that night, and they used this to carry out some of the most depraved acts of violence and torture possible.

Feeble-minded but barbaric gang leader John Travers ordered the group to drag their captive back to the car. They demanded that the woman remove her clothes, something she refused to do. Despite the evil surrounding her, she stood by her principles and stood up to her attackers. "I'm married," she told them, only to be met with laughter. Realizing that morals weren't something the group of thugs had, she changed tack and tried to put them off assaulting her by telling them she was on her period. The response to this was for the five men to begin punching Anita in the face, breaking her cheekbones and nose in the process. With blood covering her and pain searing her whole head, it was a miracle Anita was still conscious. The five brutes then demanded oral sex, something they would carry out without remorse, one after the other.

The vile quintet wasn't done yet, either. Far from it. They remembered the initial reason they targeted Anita - it was to rob her money to fill up the gas tank. After their horrific attack on their victim, they rummaged through her handbag and stole her cash. They got the fuel and raced off with the beaten victim in the back of the car, heading towards the stables at nearby Reen Road. They dragged a bloodied Anita from the car and hauled her into a paddock before resuming their attack.

She would endure multiple rapes at the hands of all five attackers here. For their own twisted pleasure, the group also continued to beat and torture Anita. For two hours, Anita was subjected to unimaginable abuse at the hands of five savages. They then dragged the badly beaten woman across some nearby barbed wire fencing, where they continued their feral acts. When they were done, Travers was vocal to the group about the fact the woman had clearly seen their faces. Not only that, the five of them had been calling each other by their real names all night, allowing Anita to not only recognize them but hand their names to the police too. It's hard to establish if it was lack of intelligence or lack of care that caused the men to be so blasé about giving their victim so much real information about them. Either way, the fact that Anita knew so much meant she had to die.

Travers was spurred on by his fellow feral criminals to murder the barely alive woman. He didn't take much convincing; after all, the man enjoyed inflicting pain on others. He used the knife he constantly carried around and slashed Anita's throat. He did this with such force, he almost decapitated her. The group then left their victim there to bleed out.

They jumped back into the stolen sedan and raced back to Travers' property. All the way there, the sick man gloated about his kill, beaming to his cohorts about how it was his first murder, relishing in how he did it. Once back home, the group opened beers and sat in Travers' garden, giddy over the events of the night. His neighbor was disrupted by an overwhelming smell seeping into her house from Travers' place. Upon further inspection, the neighbor discovered a large fire blazing, with the five beer-guzzling men standing around it. She didn't know it, but they were burning the belongings of the woman they'd just tormented, abused, and killed.

Again, it's hard to tell if this next part was stupidity or carelessness for the criminals, but they'd left their victim's body in a spot where she was bound to be found quickly. The morning after the attack, the farmer noticed his cows acting weird, and took a closer look; on the barbed fence enclosing them was a naked, beaten woman, wearing nothing but her wedding ring.

At this point, nobody was actively searching for Anita. Although her parents thought it strange their daughter hadn't come home, she was an adult. She perhaps stopped over at a friend's that night, they reasoned, although they couldn't help feeling pangs of worry. When Anita didn't show up for work, their worry was immediately warranted, and they knew something terrible had happened. The murdered woman found that morning was straight away considered to potentially be Anita. The family was shown the distinctive wedding ring found on the body, and it was confirmed that it was Anita's. Garry and Grace Lynch were beyond devastated and were yet to learn about the horrific circumstances surrounding their daughter's death. John Cobby was explained to police as being estranged from his wife and quickly found himself as suspect number one. As the investigation progressed in the days that followed, it became clear the husband was grieving just as much as the rest of her family and was cleared of any involvement.

While the investigation was taking place, a formal identification had to be carried out. Garry Lynch was taken to Westmead Mortuary, where a sheet covered the body he feared was his daughter. The white cover was pulled back to reveal a blue and purple face filled with cuts and wounds, and for a few moments, Garry couldn't be sure it was Anita. Perhaps he didn't want to believe it was her, but just as likely, he truly couldn't recognize his own daughter from the number of lacerations she had covering her head. "It's her," he finally confirmed, and in that split second, the Lynch's world crumbled around them.

February 6 rolled around, four days after the sickening crime. The murder had made it to the press, and New South Wales was in a state of shock. They didn't know the true extent of the killing, though. That would change when John Laws, a radio host, obtained a copy of Anita's autopsy report. He clutched the shocking details of the crime, mentally preparing himself to tell the nation what had truly happened the night of February 2. At times, he thought it best not to divulge this information, but eventually decided it was in the state's best interest to know what kind of sick criminals were still on the loose. The description was explicit, but there was no way around that.

Now that the residents of New South Wales knew the extent of the crime, they were incensed. They were baying for blood. Police now knew more than one person was involved in the attack and murder, and the hunt was on. The public were desperate for justice to be served, and many of them wanted to dish it out themselves.

Now that the crime was gaining traction from the public, the police got a call from the family who witnessed the abduction of Anita. Paul McGaughey was the young man who bravely scoured the streets for the white sedan Anita was dragged into, and he found it, but mistakenly believed he'd got the wrong car. It suddenly dawned on him that he had in fact found the right car, and called the police to give them any extra pieces of evidence he may unknowingly have.

A few days later, Anita's funeral took place. The church was packed and the public and those who never knew Anita personally came to pay their respects. The case had affected the state in a way few crimes had before or have since, and public outrage filled the air. Capital punishment was the preferred form of justice for the majority of locals. $50,000 was offered for any information that brought the killers to justice.

Shortly thereafter, the police received an anonymous tip-off about John Travers and his violent minions Michael Murdoch and the Murphy trio. It was in relation to the car they stole that night, that just so happened to be the same make and model Paul McGaughey pursued the evening Anita was abducted. The five were no strangers to the police, and a delve into their case files showed as much. Investigators set about arresting the group, with John Travers the first to be captured. The others were also brought in shortly after, and charged with car theft. All but Travers were released on bail. There wasn't enough evidence to detain them, but the police had a plan to get the truth out of the ringleader. He remained locked up, pending additional questioning. While they had the criminal in their clutches for a short while, investigators had to work fast. They enlisted the aid of one of Travers' family members to help secure a confession.

Although afraid of him, Travers' unnamed relative agreed to help with the investigation. In a pre-planned meet, officers taped hidden microphones to the relative and sent her into his cell under the guise of handing Travers some cigarettes. "Miss. X", as the woman was referred to, secured a full confession from the killer. He told her everything, implicating not only himself but his entire gang. Before making any arrests, police officers used Miss. X's connection with the five men to record a conversation she had with Michael Murdoch. He corroborated Travers' story, leading to police making four more swift arrests.

Yet another tip-off guided officers to the whereabouts of the men, with Gary Murphy making a run for it, only to run directly into a line of officers, who subsequently handled him to the floor with ease. To further expose his true cowardice, Gary urinated all over himself when he was placed in handcuffs. He hadn't endured anything close to what he put Anita Cobby through, yet here he was, getting escorted into a police car with his jeans covered in his urine. The press was there to capture the moment, and the image was plastered all over the New South Wales newspapers.

With the evidence presented to the five men, denying the crime was out of the question. They had Travers on tape, recounting the murder to Miss. X, laughing about the vile things he did to Anita. The recording also had Travers on tape threatening his relative to keep the confession to herself, or she'd be next. He spoke of the gruesome things every other member of the group did to their victim. Then there was the taped conversation with Murdoch. Instead of denying the crime, they all downplayed their roles and implicated one another.

One aspect they all agreed on was who the killer was. Travers admitted to the killing but insisted he was pressured to by the other members. They disagreed with this, stating Travers wanted to kill the girl and did so of his own free will.

The trial began on March 16, 1987, and in an unexpected twist, all five men pleaded guilty to the crime. The sickening details of the attack were read out for the jury to hear, although their casual laughter and chatter throughout the trial exposed the accused as the cruel and uncaring individuals they were. The autopsy report was read out, revealing the entirety of Anita's body had been beaten, including her legs, breasts, and groin. Her ear had been severed. Her bottom half had been particularly injured by the barbed wire the men dragged her across. After her throat was cut, it was revealed it took two minutes for Anita to die.

All but Travers offered a defense; as much of a defense as they could, at least. Each man minimized their participation in the beating and assaulting of Anita, and each pointed a finger at other members of the group, particularly toward Travers. Still, the public outcry was clear to see. The day of the trial saw baying crowds try to lynch the men, banging on the police van that took them to and from the court. A homemade dummy was hanging from a noose, a threat to the five criminals from an outraged, angry public. They wanted death, but that was off the table. Anita, her family, and the public, incensed on her behalf, got the next best thing: all men were found guilty of murder and sexual assault, and given life behind bars with no chance of parole.

While the result could never come close to helping the Lynch family heal, it was a small victory. Five violent, dangerous men were off the streets for the rest of their natural lives. John Cobby, understandably, struggled during the aftermath of his wife's murder. While they were separated, it looked like a reunion was on the cards for the young pair, although the couple was cruelly stripped of the chance to reconnect. John did marry again, but it didn't work out. He felt the burden of guilt for not being there for Anita, wondering what if they'd just worked things out sooner, none of this would have happened.

Garry and Grace Lynch would never be the same after Anita's death. The couple would endure decades without their beloved daughter until Garry succumbed to Alzheimer's in 2008. Grace would live another five years on her own until she passed away in 2013. Despite the struggles, heartache, and trauma they endured, they always made sure they stuck by one another, no matter how hard it was.

As for the five killers, they were sent to maximum security prisons in June 1987. Michael Murphy, the eldest of the Murphy brothers, died of cancer in 2019, aged 66. He lived a whole 40 years more than Anita was afforded by him and his gang. The remainder of the group has moved from prison to prison over the years, but the exact location of these jails is held from public knowledge.

As these men get old in jail, you have to wonder if they've found any kind of feelings of guilt or remorse for their actions. Can people like this be haunted by the atrocious acts they've committed, or do they just accept it and get on with their life? You'd think life behind bars would give you plenty of time to think and ruminate, but in the case of these individuals, it's uncertain if they have the ability to do so.

A Stranger Calls By

Cases that go unsolved for many years - often decades - tend to feel like the most frustrating ones to learn about. As true crime followers, we like to have a conclusion to the case, and preferably for justice to have been served. Cold cases leave us feeling hopeless, and doubtful that the victim and their families will ever be given the small slice of satisfaction that seeing the perpetrator behind bars would bring.

Still, unsolved crimes are sadly a huge part of true crime data, but in recent years, science has helped bring many a cold case criminal to justice. Forensics and DNA are relatively new additions to an investigator's arsenal, but they've proven to be invaluable.

Crimes that go unsolved for years (and as such, allow the criminal to roam the streets freely) are now able to be looked at retrospectively with the newfound power of DNA testing. It brings a great sense of satisfaction when a murderer or rapist finds themselves behind bars when they thought they'd got away with their despicable crime. A recent example of this is the capture of the Golden State killer. The serial criminal, culpable for dozens of murders and rapes in the 70s and 80s, left his DNA at the scene of a gruesome crime scene. This was collected and preserved with the assumption that one day, science would evolve enough to use that genetic information to link killers to their crimes.

For decades, the case was ice cold. On a wing and a prayer, in 2018 investigators put the unknown assailants' DNA into a genealogy database. From there, authorities were able to trace the killer's family, leading them to the elusive and brutal Golden State killer, who we now know as former police officer Joseph DeAngelo. He was in his early 70s when he was found guilty of murder and kidnapping, and will die behind bars.

The following case is one of those frustrating ones I was talking about
- a crime that is so bitterly cold, you don't hold out any hope it'll ever
be solved. That was until a break in DNA offered the chance to crack
the case and bring the killer to justice - but would police re-examine the
historic case in time to capture the criminal?

Angela Marie Samota, Angie to her friends, was a studious 20-year-old.
Born in California in 1964, she headed south to attend Southern
Methodist University in Dallas, Texas to study computer science. The
friendly and approachable young woman was popular with her peers,
and although she was known to dedicate a lot of her time to her studies,
she didn't shun fun times with her friends.

One such evening of fun was on October 12, 1984. Angela and two
of her friends, Anita Kadala and Russell Buchanan, set off to enjoy a
night at the annual state fair. After getting some thrills on the rides
and making the most of the copious food stalls selling corn dogs and
turkey legs, the trio decided they'd hit the Rio Room for some drinks,
dancing, and socializing. They decided to call it a night just before 1
am, and Angela drove her friends home safely before dropping in to see
her boyfriend, Ben McCall, at his apartment. Ben took a raincheck on
the night out at the fair because he had work early in the morning, but
he welcomed a quick visit from his girlfriend to say goodnight.

After checking in with Ben, Angela got back to her own apartment,
but a strange turn of events saw her call her boyfriend in a panic.
There was some stranger in her apartment, she said, and he told her
he needed to use her phone and bathroom. Angela didn't know the
person who knocked at her door to use her facilities, and he was giving
her a bad feeling. Ben was confused, and any questions he had were
cut off when Angela blurted out, "I'll call you back," before hanging

up. Understandably freaked out by the situation, Ben waited by his phone for the promised call back. It never came. He called her back, no answer. He tried again.

As the clock slowly ticked by, Ben grew more agitated about what could be going on at Angela's place. He pulled on some trousers and a sweater and jumped in his car to make his way to Angela's condo, finding the door locked and his bangs on it unanswered. The concerned man called the police to let them know he thought something bad had happened to his girlfriend. They arrived shortly after and broke down Angela's door and made their way into the apartment. Their worst fears wouldn't just be realized - they'd be exceeded.

Officers cautiously entered the apartment and made their way to her bedroom. They found Angela lying lifeless on her bed, naked, bloodied, and with stab wounds covering her body. One stab wound was so violent and had been dealt with such force that it penetrated her completely, leaving a horrific wound at the front and back of her ravaged body. Ben waited outside of the apartment as he let law enforcement do their job. When they came out to tell him the awful truth, he was devastated - but police had their eye on him as a suspect.

A subsequent autopsy of Angela found she'd been raped prior to her horrific murder. A total of 18 stab wounds were counted, the fatal injuries being deep punctures to her heart.

Police retraced Angela's final hours. The friends she attended the fair with both said they went home and went straight to sleep. Authorities found themselves drawn to Ben McCall and hauled him in for another round of questioning. He denied raping and murdering Angela, insisting he raised the alarm because she called him about an unknown man in her condo - *he* was the true killer. In a bid to get to the truth, the police suggested Ben take a lie detector test. He declined.

Exasperated, investigators suggested taking a DNA swab from Ben. DNA testing wasn't as sophisticated then as it is now. This was 1984, so the use of genetic testing in investigations was limited. But it could help rule Ben out by informing them if he was a secretor or non-secretor. In layman's terms, a secretor is an individual who secretes their blood type antigens into their bodily fluids, such as in their saliva. A non-secretor generally does not produce their blood type antigens into their fluids.

The killer was a non-secretor, the police knew that much. Around 80% of people are said to be secretors.

Investigators had no choice but to let Ben walk free as they continued with their inquiries. Testing his DNA would take a little while, so they explored other avenues while they awaited the results. Again, they found themselves speaking to Anita Kadala and Russell Buchanan, two of the last people to see her alive the morning she was murdered. Anita was shaken by the whole event but had nothing to offer investigators that would help them with the case. Russell, however, was beginning to become a bigger blip on the police's radar.

He lived just a few minutes from Angela's apartment and left town quickly after the crime became public knowledge. He was awkward and shy, and through questioning those closest to Angela, investigators discovered Russell was sweet on the 20-year-old. Whether Angela knew this or not is uncertain, but her friendship with him (on her part, at least) was based on her desire to pick his brains about his job. He was an architect, and Angela was keen to know more about how he became established in his field. He was a few years older than her and could offer her tales of firsthand experience in a role that she was keen to pursue. Still, police were interested to know that Russell thought of Angela in a more-than-friends way.

Another person investigators spoke to was Sheila Wysocki, Angela's roommate who was luckily staying at her mom's the night the murder happened. I say "luckily" - this could be viewed as a lucky or unlucky event, depending on how you see it. From one point of view, it was perhaps lucky, because Sheila managed to unknowingly keep herself out of the firing line of a violent, murderous sex attacker by staying out that night. However, what if she had made the choice to stay home that fateful evening? Would the killer have dared take on two girls, or would he have been put off by an additional person there? Could Sheila's presence have scared off the callous man who burst into their apartment asking to use the phone?

These are perhaps the questions Sheila spent a lot of time asking herself. The news of her roommate's death shook her to the core. She would be utterly devastated, and the crime consumed her thoughts. She dropped out of college. She followed the case obsessively, often meeting with investigators to obtain updates on their inquiries. Her entire life became engulfed in solving this heinous crime. In her hunt for answers, Sheila knew one thing: Russell Buchanan made her uncomfortable, and she told the police as much.

Analysis of Ben McCall's DNA showed he was a secretor, ruling him out of the suspect list. Investigators had requested DNA from Russell by this point too, which showed he was a non-secretor, just like the killer. This wasn't enough evidence to make an arrest, but Sheila wanted to do her own investigative work. So, she invited Russell out for some lunch to try to coax some information out of him or catch him in a lie.

As Sheila sat opposite the person she suspected of killing her friend, she was overwhelmed by the idea she was staring at the very man who raped and mutilated her roommate. Russell had willingly taken a lie detector, which showed he was telling the truth when he denied murdering

Angela. However, a further look into the results showed Russell was being deceptive, thus making Sheila even more on edge when talking to the man.

During the lunch, Russell told Sheila that he'd done countless interviews with police and that they kept bringing him in for questioning. In the end, it seemed investigators had got as much as they were going to get from Russell, who decided to stop cooperating with the investigation.

It soon got back to Sheila that Russell had got himself a lawyer - not just any lawyer, though. He'd enlisted the services of Richard Haynes. Haynes was renowned for taking on the cases of the out-and-out guilty. Russell didn't help himself or quell people's opinion that he was Angela's killer, but surprisingly, Sheila was exploring other avenues by this point. There was no evidence, other than heavy suspicion, to arrest Russell. Sheila had to move on to other possibilities with the little to no evidence there was.

Decades passed with no crack in the case. Sheila still hounded the investigators from time to time, kept printouts of the crime from newspapers, and kept a dossier of similar rapes that occurred in the area around the same time as Angela's murder. By this point, it was 2004, a full 20 years since the gruesome crime. Frustrated with the lack of movement in the case, Sheila, on a whim, made a big decision: she was going to become a private investigator. In her early 40s, she retrained in her new profession, studying as hard and as much as she could - just like Angela did all those years ago. Angela never got the chance to fulfill her dream career. Sheila was going to take this opportunity with both hands to finally bring the killer to justice.

It would be a difficult task ahead of her, though. The case was cold - frozen, in fact. Still, she hounded the Dallas Police Department, suspecting she rang their number in the region of 700 times. While she never got a callback, Sheila suspected her persistent calls caused fed-up investigators to reexamine Angela's case.

It was now 2008, and Detective Linda Crum was given the task of opening up Angela's cold case. Authorities had collected DNA from under Angela's fingernails, a clear indication that the woman had fought back before being savaged by the killer. There were also semen samples, and some blood collected, and these vital pieces of evidence were finally put through the DNA system that held the information of criminals.

In 2009, Sheila received a phone call from investigators. "We got him." It was the call she'd been waiting 25 years to hear. She waited for the officer to follow up with, "It was Russell all along," but they didn't. "It's Donald Bess." A wave of confusion hit Sheila; she'd never heard of him. *Who was Donald Bess?*

Career criminal Bess was well known to authorities. He was a serial sex offender who, at the time of his DNA being matched to Angela's crime scene, was out on parole for some pretty nasty offenses: kidnapping and rape. Bess, nicknamed "The Beast" by Sheila, was brought in for questioning. Immediately, he denied any involvement. He never hurt any of his victims like that, he said. Mid-interview, Bess asked detectives a strange question: "Does this have something to do with Dallas?" An interesting comment for someone who purported to have no involvement in the murder. Investigators' ears pricked up, but Bess immediately shut down. He refused any more questioning.

It looked like some investigative work was in order since Bess wasn't speaking. Police found that the serial sex pest was out on parole at the time Angela was killed - and traced him back to Dallas at the time the murder took place. Although Donald Bess denied culpability, there was too much evidence stacked against him. Investigators surmised that Bess saw Angela making her way to her condo that night and took his chance, conning his way into her property by saying he needed to use the phone. Then, he pounced, before leaving her butchered corpse on the very bed he indecently assaulted her on.

If the abundance of forensic evidence against Bess wasn't enough, news of his arrest spread through the town, and a plethora of women came forward to tell the police about their terrifying experiences with "The Beast." One of them was his ex-wife, who told of a marriage filled with violence and abuse, explaining how he not only beat her but their child, too. Other women had similar stories of being raped by Bess, and they testified against him at his trial for Angela's murder. Collectively, they were Angela's voice.

In June 2008, 60-year-old Bess was found guilty of Angela's rape and murder and was given the death penalty. Finally, justice had been served, and Sheila was one of the many people in attendance who breathed a sigh of relief that a serial sexual deviant was off the streets. Of course, Bess appealed his sentence, which was swiftly dismissed.

After the trial, Sheila felt she had to tie up some loose ends and right some wrongs; namely, she wanted to speak with Russell Buchanan. For decades, she hated this man, and vilified him, assuming him guilty of her friend's murder. After all, he failed a lie detector (which isn't always reliable, as we can see here), and he began stonewalling investigators. Sheila called him up and asked to meet up. The pair visited Angela's grave together, where Sheila offered Russell an apology. Here, the pair gained mutual closure. For Russell, the weight of blame and assumed guilt lifted from his shoulders, and for Sheila, she got to see the true killer face justice and make amends with the person she'd suspected all these years.

Donald Bess never made it to the chair. He died behind bars in late 2022 from a heart attack aged 74. Unknowingly, from beyond the grave, Angela managed to bring her killer to justice. She potentially spared other women from his clutches and brought closure to his dozens of victims by seeing him locked up until his death.

A Consensual Killing

You've read the title and are perhaps feeling a little perplexed. Can you ever consent to your own murder? It seems Sharon Lopatka did, aged just 35 when she left her home for the last time to meet a man she'd met online. Together, they agreed she would be tortured and murdered by his hand. Victor Lopatka, her husband, had no clue of his wife's dark desires and secret life online. The day she left the marital home, on October 13, 1996, she left Victor a letter. In it, she explained she wouldn't be returning. This wasn't just any *"Dear John"* letter, though; Sharon told her husband, "If my body is never retrieved, don't worry."

Victor immediately called the police, hoping they could track down his wife and save her from herself. They would be too late.

Up until that point, Sharon was viewed as unassuming, described as being "as normal as you can get" by one of her high school classmates. She married Victor as a teenager, although by some accounts this wasn't a marriage born out of young love, but rather an act of teen rebellion on Sharon's part. She'd been raised by strict religious parents who were unhappy when their daughter eloped with a young construction worker. The newly married couple eventually set up home in Hampstead, Maryland, a sleepy suburban town with rows of tract homes and residents who knew mostly everyone else who lived there.

While this wasn't the life her parents had in mind for Sharon, she would go on to be a successful entrepreneur. She capitalized on the dot-com boom of the early 90s, starting online businesses before a lot of people even knew what that meant.

She began her foray into online entrepreneurship, selling interior design guides for a few dollars each. Her website would collect payment from customers and Sharon would mail them their guide in the post, promising them "quick, easy ways to decorate your home." In 1995, this was a fairly new concept for entrepreneurs, and Sharon maximized the internet as much as she could by starting another online business, this time managing sites that offered psychic readings. She would be paid a percentage of sales made by promoting various psychic phone numbers.

While this brought in money, it seemed that being in front of the computer all day was becoming more than for money-making purposes. Soon, Sharon found her way to pornographic forums, initially selling her own worn items of clothing under the pseudonym "Nancy Carlson." Victor was completely unaware of his wife's newfound life on the internet, which was quickly consuming her. Sharon, as Nancy Carlson, trawled forums online, ones that focused on fetishes and sadomasochistic acts. The internet, and the individuals on those forums, fed Sharon's desires; ones her husband had no idea she was harboring. From necrophilia to foot fetishism, Sharon was a regular in these types of chat rooms. Or rather, Nancy was.

"Nancy" was a 300-pound adult film actress who specialized in torture. That's how Sharon described her, anyway. Sharon was about half that size, but held desires of being a "gainer" - someone who enjoys being fed until they gain an unhealthy amount of weight. She would speak to "feeders" - individuals who enjoy watching the gainer put on weight. She was also speaking to various other members of fetish forums about the idea of her being tortured to death. Eventually, this led to Sharon putting out requests for someone to volunteer to do just that.

Six hours away in North Carolina, Robert Glass was sitting behind his computer screen in his unkempt home, logging into the very chatrooms Sharon was frequenting. Robert was recently divorced, with his use of the internet being the catalyst for his wife leaving him. Sherri Glass had been getting frustrated with Robert's constant need to be online and found it had created a divide in their marriage. Not only that, it meant Robert was neglecting his three young children in order to surf the web, so one day when her husband was away from the family computer - an unusual occurrence - she logged into his email account. What she found would cause the world she knew to crash around her.

Robert wasn't just innocently browsing the web - he was viewing violent and sadistic sites of a sexual nature. Sherri had no idea her husband was into the kind of stuff he had saved on his computer. On top of this, Robert was also exchanging messages and emails to other women about his fetishes, using the names "Slowhand" and "Toyman", depending on what forums he was using. After this startling discovery, Sherri packed up and took the kids, leaving Robert with just his internet companions.

On August 6, 1996, Robert logged into his chat rooms as usual and got talking to a new woman: Sharon Lopatka. The steamy chats soon spilled over to email exchanges, and the next two months would see the pair swap hundreds of emails. Printed out, these made up 900 pages of talk of torture and death. This led to the conversation of Sharon being tortured to death. Robert would be the obliging torturer, unlike many other men who'd engage in this type of chat with Sharon, only to back out of acting out in real life. Quite the contrary in this instance: Robert was more than happy to fulfill their shared fantasy.

Sharon had been actively looking for someone to "torture her until death," as she advertised it. She posted on these forums that she'd love to email someone who was willing to do this. At one point, an individual scouring these chatrooms would reach out to Sharon and try to talk her out of her plan. Sharon rebuffed the stranger's attempt to help her, instead scolding the woman for "preaching" to her.

Robert's and Sharon's chats had escalated to the point where they were ready to meet, and the date was set. October 13 would be the day Sharon would get to fulfill her fantasy.

That fateful October morning had started out like any other for Victor Lopatka until he was stopped in his tracks when he found a handwritten note laid out for him. He thought his wife had merely headed out to meet a friend; that's what she told him, anyway. He unfolded the note, and after trying to digest its content, called the police. They arrived at the Lopatka residence and found that while Victor had little in the way of any clues to his wife's whereabouts, her computer would divulge all of her deepest secrets. This would offer even more trauma and heartache for Victor to absorb, as well as the notion that he might never see his wife ever again.

Meanwhile, Sharon was well on her way to meeting Robert. By the time the police arrived, she was already on the train to Charlotte, where Robert would pick her up and drive her to his home. Once there, behind closed doors, only Robert can say what really happened. As agreed, Sharon ended up dead, but Robert would change his story when police caught up with him days after Sharon left her home for the last time.

Days passed before the police found their way to Robert's home. A search of the property found human remains in a shallow grave near his house. With an abundance of evidence - not least a dead body close to his home - the police made their arrest. The body was identified as Sharon, and a subsequent autopsy found she died by strangulation, but surprisingly found no sign of torture. That was the whole point of the meeting if the email exchanges were anything to go by. Sharon explicitly said she wanted to die via torture. Robert explicitly explained how he would do this. After being hauled into the interrogation room, Robert pleaded, "I never wanted to kill her," as he told police how the death was an accident. It seemed Robert was trying to convince authorities that this was a consensual game gone wrong, something the emails contradicted.

Some people believed Robert, seeing as there were no signs of the promised torture to Sharon's body. According to Robert, while they slept together, he engaged in consensual asphyxiation with Sharon only to find she stopped breathing completely. He then buried her a stone's throw away from his house.

Other people rebuffed Robert's version of events as lies, suggesting he was merely covering his tracks. To them, he was a cold-blooded killer who preyed on a vulnerable woman. Some people were on the fence, confused as to how or why a person would want to die in this manner.

An aspect of this case that will never be discovered is Sharon's reason for desiring to die in such a horrific way. There is a rare phenomenon of people who seek to be slaughtered by their sexual partner, but as most people don't understand this way of thinking, they could only conclude that Sharon was depressed and wanted to end her life. She was known to harm herself from time to time, and her unhappiness surrounding her marriage was clear to see from the comments she made to her online acquaintances. However, her neighbors viewed her as a "happy" person, albeit quiet, and viewed the Lopatkas as your typical, content couple. As we know, outside appearances can be deceiving, and we never truly know what's going on behind closed doors. We can see that Sharon tried to play the part of a happy wife, to the local residents at least. The community was shocked by the revelation that their neighbor had died, and even more speechless when they found out the circumstances of her death.

Robert Glass was maintaining his innocence in murdering Sharon, still insisting he didn't mean to end her life. This was an unusual case for authorities because if Robert was telling the truth, it was a gray area that wasn't easy to navigate. It's morally and lawfully known that someone can't consent to their own death unless it's a special circumstance, such as euthanasia, which raises a separate debate of its own. But Sharon wasn't dying, nor was she suffering any known mental health issues. In the end, Robert would plead guilty to voluntary manslaughter. However, he would also find himself with a plethora of other charges against him, after investigators found a stash of illegal items in his home.

Found among the strewn bondage items and toys, explicit magazines, and weapons were vile images involving children. He ended up pleading guilty to sexual exploitation alongside manslaughter. For Sharon's death, he got 36-53 months behind bars, and for the illegal images, he got a further 27 months. On January 27, 2000, he was locked up, but he'd not serve his full - some say lenient - sentence. He died in 2002 of a heart attack.

This tale is truly undefinable when it comes to categorizing it as a true crime case. The victim seemingly wanted to die, and the killer carried out a murder much less violent than the victim seemingly desired. Sharon sadly lost her life in her pursuit of fulfillment, but who knows if it's truly what she wanted? This tale is sure to divide opinion on who was to blame, or whether Sharon was even a victim at all. The only person who knew what went on that tragic October day was Robert, and any additional information he had about Sharon's frame of mind or desires went with him to the grave.

Irreconcilable Differences

Marriages have ups and downs. Any married person, at one point or another, will butt heads with their significant other, and occasionally feel the odd pangs of frustration or anger towards their spouse. In cases where the differences are just too extreme to overcome, divorce tends to be the option of choice. For Dalia Dippolito, the resentment she felt for her husband drove her to hire a hitman to get him out of her life - by ending his.

New York-born Dalia had a stable upbringing in the city, eventually moving to Boynton Beach, Florida with her parents and brother and sister when she was a teenager. She would finish high school here, graduating in 2000. The 18-year-old was keen to build a career and earn some money, but she didn't know what she wanted to do. Eventually, she settled in real estate but took on the role of an escort when the sun went down. Money was often tight growing up, particularly when her parents split after their move to Florida, and Dalia wanted to make sure she had an abundance of money now that she was old enough to earn her own.

The escorting gig proved to be fruitful, paying more than her real estate job. That same year, she met Michael Dippolito when he booked her for an evening. He wouldn't end up being just another client - he was immediately struck by Dalia and felt she certainly wasn't just another escort. Even though Michael was already married, he professed his love for Dalia. Michael quickly left his wife to be with his new love, and married Dalia on February 2, 2009. This was mere days after his divorce had been finalized, but the whirlwind romance caused Michael to become blind to any red flags Dalia Dippolito had been exhibiting.

Mike, as he preferred to be called, was an ex-convict, out on probation for fraud. This was something he was trying to put behind him, until shortly after his marriage to Dalia, when his probation officer came knocking at his door. This worried Mike, considering he'd never had a visit from the probation team since his release from prison. Anxious to know why the officer felt the need to come to his home, he questioned the unexpected and unannounced drop-in. The probation officer informed Mike that his office had received a number of calls about illegal drugs being sold from his property. This was news to Mike, and he told the officer as much. Still, his probation officer had come armed with a warrant, and a search of Mike's house was carried out.

While his house was being foraged for the steroids and ecstasy he was accused of selling, Mike was a bundle of fear. Not because he had any drugs in the home, but because any small run-in with the law would see him sent back to jail for another decade. After what seemed like an eternity, officers told Mike the home was clean, and no further action was going to be taken.

The following week, Dalia suggested the couple take a break and have a relaxing weekend away together. They headed to Palm Beach where their romantic getaway was abruptly halted by a police patrol car waiting for Mike in the hotel parking lot. They ordered him out of his vehicle so they could search his car. There had been reports he was selling illegal substances from his car and police were required to do a thorough search to ensure he wasn't breaking his parole conditions. Again, an anxious and perplexed Mike let officers rummage through his belongings, understandably concerned that someone was trying to set him up. Again, the police found nothing in their search, and Mike was free to go.

He was comforted by Dalia, who also questioned what was going on and who was possibly trying to set her husband up. The following week, the pair enjoyed a meal at a high-end restaurant, hoping their run-ins with the police were over. After settling the bill, the pair headed to the parking lot to drive home but were stopped in their tracks by a patrol car. "Not again," Mike said, exasperated with the constant police presence in his life despite now being on the straight and narrow. Yet again, officers wanted to search his vehicle as he'd been reported for dealing drugs. Mike allowed another search of his car, but this time, officers found something: a bag of cocaine in his cigarette pack. Tears streamed from Mike as he pleaded his case with officers, insisting the drugs weren't his and he had no idea how they got there. He knew this meant he was going back to prison, but worse than that, he was going to prison for something he definitely wasn't guilty of.

Astonishingly, though, the police were inclined to believe Michael. Despite the evidence suggesting otherwise, the police went off their gut instinct and let Mike go free. His emotional reaction to the drugs being found, coupled with the strange "hiding" place they were in, caused police to be suspicious that he was perhaps being set up. Plus, his wife merely stood there almost emotionless as her husband had a breakdown. This didn't go unnoticed: not by officers and not by Mike himself.

After processing the trauma of potentially facing prison time again, Mike began to think logically: his wife was the only person who knew their whereabouts that night. "Did you have anything to do with the police turning up tonight?" he asked Dalia, who was sitting in stone-cold silence in the driver's seat. Incensed by her husband's questioning, Dalia became angry, screaming and shouting at Mike for even thinking she was to blame. The riled-up woman then began driving erratically, causing Mike to recant his accusations in order for her to calm down.

Despite his doubts, Mike believed his wife. Perhaps because he wanted to believe she wouldn't behave so nefariously, or perhaps because she was such a convincing liar. In reality, his worst fears had been realized: the person he loved had been calling the police in order to set him up. Still, Mike reasoned to himself, *why would she want to do that? What would she gain from it?*

Life carried on as normal, and the calls to the police about Mike's drug dealing business seemed to stop. However, Dalia had changed tactics. Setting her husband up was too risky now, so she contacted an ex, also called Mike. Dalia had used this ex for money before dumping him, but he was always available if she ever needed him. In this instance, she had a strange request from him, in exchange for some "alone time" with her. Dalia wanted Mike to call her husband and pretend to be a lawyer, and convince Micheal of the benefits of moving all his assets into his wife's name. Mike - portraying himself as a lawyer - called Dalia's husband and reminded him that he was on probation, offering him all the beneficial reasons to make sure his assets were safe by handing them over to his wife.

The call sounded legit to Mike, who went ahead with the "lawyers" advice. Michael Dippolito handed his house over to Dalia within days of the call.

Part one of Dalia's plan had been executed. Part two was about to be set in motion when she contacted another ex, Mohamed Shihadeh. She met up with her former lover and confided in him that she needed a hitman to kill her husband. She asked for Mohamed's help in obtaining one before they parted ways. It looked like part two of Dalia's evil plan was going smoothly until Mohamed did something Dalia surely didn't expect: he took this information straight to the police station. He told them everything he knew about his ex wanting to end her husband's life and was willing to help them snare the malevolent woman.

Small, undetectable cameras were placed in Mohamed's car, complete with microphones. Police needed irrefutable evidence that Mohamed was telling the truth, and a taped meeting of Dalia admitting to wanting her husband killed would solidify the case.

Mohamed arranged his next meeting with Dalia in his car, on July 30, 2009, which captured a wealth of evidence against the woman. Not only did Dalia hand her ex a picture of Mike to give to the hitman, but she also paid him thousands of dollars as a deadly deposit to secure her husband's demise. A few days later, Dalia would meet with the "hitman" - aka Widy Jean, a narcotics officer at Boynton Beach Police Department. "How soon can we get everything going?" Dalia coldly asked the man she believed to be her husband's killer. When he replied it was up to her, she insisted she needed "it done this week." The hitman promised to deliver "two in the head" to Mike the following Wednesday before staging a break-in at their home. Before parting ways, the hitman warned Dalia that once they say their goodbyes, there'll be no more contact, so she won't have the chance to change her mind. She assured him that she had no intention of changing her mind.

On the morning of Wednesday, August 5, 2009, Dalia headed to the gym. Not out of the norm, but today she was heading there for more than just a workout - she was heading there to provide a CCTV alibi of where she was at the time her husband was murdered. She expected that by the time she arrived home, her husband would have had "two in the head" as promised, and she would be heading for a life of luxury with her entrepreneur husband's assets all to herself.

After a workout, Dalia drove back home. As she pulled up outside the marital home that morning, police surrounded the property, tape cornered off the entrance to the house, and officers were pacing outside as forensics collected their evidence. It was a sight straight out of a detective drama, and drama is exactly what officers at the scene got:

Dalia was hysterical when she was told her husband had been killed. It was all caught on camera, too, via officers' body cams. She fell into the arms of the officer who notified her of Mike's death, screaming, "No," repeatedly as she cried. This footage is available online, and if we didn't know any better, we would believe that Dalia was a distraught wife who was heartbroken over the sudden and brutal loss of her husband. But, we do know better - and the whole charade is difficult to watch, mainly because of the high-school drama class acting.

Police advised the grief-stricken widow that she needed to come to the station to discuss who her husband knew that might want to kill him. She begged to see Mike but was warned that she definitely didn't want to see him after the ordeal he'd endured at the killer's hands. "Is there any reason why someone would want to kill your husband?" the investigator asked. Quick as a flash, Dalia began recanting Mike's criminal history, painting him as a serial lawbreaker with a stack of enemies who may want him out of the picture. By this point, the crying and hysterics had miraculously stopped, and Dalia was talking to officers matter-of-factly.

Suddenly, in the middle of questioning, the interrogating officer opened the door of the small room he was sitting in with Dalia. "Get over here," he demanded to an unknown presence outside the room. Escorted by another officer, a handcuffed, meek-looking Widy Jean walked into the interrogation room, still playing the role of the hitman. "Do you know who this guy is?" the interrogator asked Dalia while pointing at Widy. "I've never seen him before," she replied with vigor. The hitman also acted as he'd never seen Dalia in his life, keeping up the ruse. "What were you doing coming out of her house?" the hitman was asked, to which there was no reply. He was quickly escorted out of the room, by which time Dalia was given a line I'm sure she'll never forget: "You're going to jail today," the interrogating officer said in a deadpan tone.

Her scheming had caught up with her, but it took Dalia a little while to catch on. Perhaps it was the deadpan way in which she was told, or perhaps it was because Dalia had never been told "no" before, but she wasn't quite getting the gravity of the situation. To help her understand, the interrogating officer told her that the hitman was in fact an undercover cop. Her husband hadn't been killed at all - he was alive and well, albeit devastated that his wife was intent on having him killed. She insisted she hadn't done anything wrong, but was informed that everything had been recorded. Again, she repeated she didn't do anything, but it was repeated to her that everything she told the undercover officer had been recorded - they had pictures, videos, and recordings to prove her guilt. The hysterical tears began again as Dalia denied any wrongdoing.

After cuffing the crying woman, officers let Mike enter the room, where Dalia would feign surprise at seeing him alive. She begged her husband to come over to see her, which he refused, telling her, "I can't fix this." Dalia was subsequently charged with solicitation of first-degree murder.

As she sat behind bars, she was given the chance to make one phone call - she chose to call Mike. She still denied plotting his murder. She needed his help, she said and asked him for an attorney. When Mike demanded answers, she refused to tell him on the phone, insisting he come to see her in jail. When she got nowhere with Mike, Dalia called her mother, who offered her comfort and promises of an attorney. "Mike did this to me," she cried to her mom. "I want him out of my house," she demanded shamelessly.

Dalia's trial began in 2011, and the tale - somehow - got even more bizarre. Despite the tall stack of evidence against her, Dalia denied any wrongdoing and even had a defense argument.

She claimed that Mike was a hopeless reality TV fanatic who was desperate to star in his own show. Dalia's defense explained that she and her husband had concocted this "murder for hire" stunt to propel Mike into the limelight, where he always wanted to be. Mike denied this, insisting the first he'd heard of it was when the police contacted him and told him about his wife's plot to end his life.

The defense argument was quickly dismissed and Dalia Dippolito was found guilty of solicitation of first-degree murder. She was handed 20 years behind bars. However, this wouldn't stick. In 2014, it was determined that the jury in this trial was improperly selected, causing a retrial to take place in 2016. She was allowed to remain under house arrest until the retrial took place, seemingly swerving the retribution her husband greatly wanted. A hung jury resulted in another mistrial, with the final trial taking place in 2017, by which time Dalia had given birth to a little boy.

She was handed 16 years in jail. Her immediate appeal was rejected, and her release date is set for 2032, with the possibility of parole taken off the table.

Despite being a "nervous wreck" in the aftermath of the trial, Mike has since moved on and has found love again with a woman named Gloria. While he says he sometimes finds it hard to trust, he admits he feels lucky to be alive in order to have met his new lover.

Mike's fate could so easily have been different if Dalia had managed to carry out her devious plot. Who knows what the alternate outcome would have been: would Mike have managed to fight off the hitman, killing him instead, securing his life behind bars? If Mike had been killed that Wednesday morning, would Dalia have been captured for her crime, or would she have lived a life of luxury as she'd anticipated? We can ponder on this, but thankfully, we'll never know what the alternative outcome would have been. In a true crime rarity, the victim not only escaped with his life but also got the last laugh in a case that could have been so much more disastrous.

He Called Himself "The Gaffer"

The tragic tale I'm about to cover has a very thin case file from which to derive information. There is little out there about the crime, and the culprit of the decades-long illegal activity has never been named in order to protect his victims' identities. I'll tread carefully, avoiding any information that may uncover the identities of the victims while outlining the deplorable actions of the perpetrator.

This horrendous story took place in Sheffield, England, in the early 80s. Back then, Sheffield was propped up by the steel and coal industries, and hardworking men would spend their spare pounds in the working men's clubs of an evening. Some of the locals would agree it was a simpler time for many working-class families back then: kids made their own entertainment. Food and clothing were scarce, meaning they were appreciated and never went to waste. There were four TV channels to choose from, not four thousand. A simpler time, perhaps, but also a time where many people wouldn't dare question what went on behind the closed doors of their neighbors' homes - not to anyone outside of their family home at least.

Today, if we suspect a family across the street is doing something illicit, we have means to back up our suspicions. We can record any strange sounds or happenings with our smartphones in order to hand over to the authorities should we conclude bad things are happening. Many of us have cameras outside our homes to capture criminal activity, complete with date and timestamp. Generally, we're all more aware of bad things happening around us, and more inclined to do something if we suspect as much. In this case, not only was the perpetrator suspected of raping and abusing his own children, there was plentiful evidence to suggest he was doing so, but nobody stopped the vile man in his tracks. Not neighbors, not social services, and not the police. His reign of terror lasted decades, but no doubt for his victims, it'll stay with them for their entire lives.

He was named the "British Fritz" when his crimes came to light. You'll perhaps recognize the name Fritzl from a high-profile case from 2008, whereby Austrian Josef Fritzl was arrested for keeping his daughter, Elisabeth Fritzl, captive in his cellar for two and a half decades. While locked up, Elisabeth was subjected to sexual assaults and abuse from her father, which resulted in her having seven children, some of which Josef took to his wife in the main house to raise. It's reported that the wife had no idea what her husband was up to, and believed him when he told her that the babies were left at the doorstep with a note from Elisabeth asking them to take care of her child. Josef was secretive about his cellar, and his wife never stepped foot in it.

Elisabeth finally managed to escape when one of her children became so sick they needed hospital care. Josef eventually let Elisabeth out of the cellar to see her sick child in hospital - the first time she'd been allowed out in 24 years since he'd locked her up when she turned 18. Nurses suspected something was amiss, and after promising Elisabeth she'd never need to see Josef again if she told them what had been going on, she told authorities everything. Fritzl was jailed for life for rape, kidnapping, and slavery, among other things.

The case of the "British Fritzl" has many similarities to the Austrian one. One big, and frustrating, difference is that there were more opportunities in this case where the culprit could have been caught a lot sooner than he was.

"The Gaffer", as he called himself, was a menacing figure in the Sheffield neighborhood he resided in. His nickname was something local residents and his own family referred to him as. Gaffer means "the boss" in British slang, someone who rules over everyone else without question. Your superior at work would be called gaffer, or some jokingly call their wife "the gaffer."

His overpowering presence caused his family to fear him, and for good reason, too. If something displeased him, he wasn't averse to beating his children, something he did regularly.

His two daughters had no chance against their repressive father. While they'd always suffered physical abuse at the hands of the person they knew as The Gaffer, the things they had to endure escalated when the girls were eight and ten, respectively. He forced himself upon them, starting a campaign of abuse that would last for years.

The wicked man would terrorize his children in the middle of the night, shouting their names to wake them from their sleep, causing them to freeze at the idea they'd be abused again. Sometimes, the man would wipe fake blood on their bedroom doors in the night to ensure his kids were constantly riddled with fear the moment they woke up. The rapes would happen almost every single day.

Should the girls try to refuse their father's sick abuse, he would threaten to kill them. They had a gas fire the man would use as a weapon, holding his daughter's faces against the grill of the scolding fireplace as they pleaded for him to stop. He warned them that if they ever told anybody about what was happening, he'd kill them both.

Between the late 80s and 2002, the girls became pregnant every single year. Sometimes, both of them became pregnant at the same time. A total of 19 pregnancies arose as a result of a sick father's desires. I use the term father here, although it's clear he never was a father, but rather a beastly presence in the two girls' lives.

The sister's mother left the family home in 1992, unable to cope with the abuse and violence she suffered at the hands of her husband. She left her children with the man she was afraid of, someone she described as having a "short fuse." With his wife taking herself out of the picture, the despicable father turned his attention solely toward his helpless young daughters.

Out of the 19 pregnancies the girls had between them, seven children survived. Five of the pregnancies ended in miscarriage, likely as a result of the abuse and emotional turmoil the girls had to endure. The girls - teenagers by this point - also had several terminations. Two of the babies would die shortly after their birth. Despite the tragic circumstances around their pregnancies, it was still a traumatic and upsetting experience for the girls to lose their babies.

There was no way out of the sick yearly ritual of getting pregnant - the malignant father would refuse to allow his daughters to take contraceptive pills. The idea of him taking precautions to stop his children from giving birth to his children (and technically his grandchildren) didn't enter his brain. In fact, it's been suggested that he took great pleasure in the suffering the difficult pregnancies caused. One of the babies born prematurely sadly died and was disposed of in an unbelievably cold manner; the fetus was flushed down the toilet.

The reason this case has been likened to the Fritzl case isn't just because of the unnatural abuse, but because the girls were also isolated from the outside world. Not in the same way as Elisabeth Fritzl, who was locked in a cellar, but they were kept in the family home and refused the opportunity to go to school. At first, they attended school irregularly; when they were sporting visible cuts and bruises, they were kept home so they didn't arouse suspicion. Later, they moved home rapidly to ensure neighbors didn't get too suspicious of the father and his two girls, who seemed to be constantly giving birth despite being so young and not having partners. Almost 40 moves, from council home to council home, saw the teenagers stripped of any ability to form relationships with their neighbors or peers.

Every time the girls had to attend the hospital for their latest pregnancy, doctors would ask for the paternity of the father. It had been noticed that the children they'd given birth to had distinct features and illnesses that pointed toward genetic disorders caused by having parents who were related. Still, the doctors or any agencies who could help the girls didn't probe further - they merely suggested that the teenagers stopped having children with whoever the father was. If only they'd explored a bit deeper, they'd understand they weren't willingly getting pregnant, but rather their father had been carrying out a campaign of abuse over his children for as long as they could remember.

While medics strongly suspected the girls' dad of being at least in some way complicit with his daughter's continued pregnancies, they didn't try to unearth the truth. They were sent back to be with their father each and every visit they made. When the girls turned up for school with visible bruises and nasty-looking injuries, teachers were concerned. Their hygiene was also something teachers noted wasn't taken care of, which was another red flag. When youngsters reach a certain age, they begin to try to take care of themselves a bit better, often pruning themselves or being overly conscious as to how they look. For the daughters of The Gaffer, they were afforded no such luxuries as they entered adulthood.

Despite him constantly keeping his family on the move, some neighbors did begin to become suspicious of the situation. In the UK at the time, child cruelty was often reported to an organization called the NSPCC (the National Society for the Prevention of Cruelty to Children), where anonymous tipsters or victims themselves could call

he helpline number to seek help. On six different occasions, members
of the public called the NSPCC about their concerns over the man
hey knew as The Gaffer. Next to nothing happened as a result of these
calls. While social workers were notified of the poor conditions the
children were growing up in, little in the way of actual help was offered
o the girls.

n the late 70s and early 80s, when the family still included the girls'
mother, social services tried to gain entry into the home but were met
with hostility from the children's parents. It was also noted how the
ocial workers who tried to liaise with the family were scared of the
menacing father, who ruled with violence and fear. The blatant injuries
he children had were clearly not accidental - despite being explained
as such - but no charges were brought against their "caregivers." As a
result, the girls continued to live a life of unimaginable cruelty and fear,
as well as abject poverty.

By all accounts, The Gaffer was work-shy, relying on state benefits to
fund his drunken lifestyle. As the girls continued having more children,
child benefits began rolling in, further propping up the man's slothful
existence. The girls would give their father the benefits they received,
which he would squander down the pub or on bottles of whisky. His
daughters hoped by handing him their money, he'd drink himself into
a state where he was incapable of abusing them. In the end, they hoped
he'd eventually drink himself to death; that seemed to be the only way
out for them.

Authorities were aware the family had problems, not least domestic
abuse and alcohol abuse, but the effects of this on his children weren't
considered. Instead, The Gaffer was left to do whatever he pleased.

How would his reign of terror ever end? If no one was willing to help,
how would the girls - by this point women - ever escape the hell they
were in? It seemed like the terrified daughters were resigned to a life of

constant abuse and emotional control. By 2008, when the women were in their 30s, help would finally arrive. It took one of the victims to come forward to crumble The Gaffer's coercive powers and for some kind of justice to be brought his way.

As it often does, history repeated itself with the abused women's children; the sisters found themselves on social services' radar due to the way they took care of their babies. This time, however, they were a constant in their lives, truly concerned about the living situation of the seven young children. Social workers would be more persistent and insistent on being involved with the family than they were decades earlier, though. Eventually, one social worker, in particular, gained one of the women's trust enough for her to tell her the truth about the situation.

By this point, the women had managed to form relationships away from their father and had met men they wanted to spend their lives with. They had managed to divulge their traumatic past to their partners, which in turn gave them the confidence to tell their social worker about everything The Gaffer had been putting them through. The women had feared they wouldn't be believed, alongside the violent repercussions they'd receive at the hands of their father should they expose him. But they knew they had to try to get him as far away from their children as possible, and getting him locked up for his heinous crimes was the only way.

The Gaffer was arrested and predictably denied the crimes. It's hard to understand how he thought his denials would be believed since DNA was now a thing and could quite easily and conclusively tell investigators if he was the father of his daughter's children. Of course, once the DNA tests were back, there was no refuting what The Gaffer had been doing to his daughters all these years.

The trial set off in 2008, and the cowardly man refused to step out in public and listen to the abhorrent list of crimes he'd committed over the decades. He was brought to Sheffield Crown Court but refused to walk to the dock, instead hiding in the confines of a cell. Such a weak display from a man who once demanded to be called The Gaffer; how the tide had turned after all these years. His once feeble and fearful daughters had now found their strength and their sick abuser was sitting sniveling in a cell, unable to hear the wicked, twisted catalog of abuse he'd carried out over the course of his life.

The jury had to sit through an abundance of evidence brought against the man, starting from his violent outbursts toward his children that led to him eventually sexually abusing them. As the kids grew older, they were seen less and less out of the family home and were isolated from making friends with other children from the estate. The handful of times they were allowed out, it was noted they appeared withdrawn and browbeat, particularly when their father was nearby. When The Gaffer was around, his daughters apparently looked scared to death. Sadly, we now know why that was. The other children found the sisters "weird", describing them as such through childhood right up to adulthood. Again, sadly, we now know why that appeared to be the case.

The jury was told how the children were denied schooling if their injuries were too obvious, how the abuse would take place every day, and how almost 20 pregnancies occurred as a result of the man's abuse.

The mother, who was in the picture until the girls were in their teens - years into the vile abuse they were subjected to - was questioned by police, too. Authorities wanted to figure out if she'd known about the abuse and done nothing about it, but despite their suspicions, were unable to formally charge her with anything. Still, she was there when one of her daughters gave birth to her grandchild at a young age. She was around when The Gaffer beat and attacked his daughters relentlessly. She was in the house as her daughters were attacked by their father in unimaginable ways. The police weren't able to prove she knew, though, and the mother eventually fled to another part of the country.

The defendant's barrister didn't deny the man's crimes - how could he with such irrefutable evidence - but he did lay the blame elsewhere. Where were social services when this abuse was taking place, he asked the courtroom, a question they were no doubt asking themselves. Still, social services weren't to blame for the abuse the children suffered. Only one person is responsible for that, and he couldn't even show his face.

The Gaffer was given a lengthy prison term, 19 years and 6 months. Perhaps behind bars, he won't have such a powerful, self-assigned nickname. It's unlikely he'll reveal his reason for incarceration to his fellow inmates, and since the case was so hidden from public knowledge, his fellow felons won't be able to research him. Still, he's away from the people he so cruelly tortured for decades, giving them the breathing room and freedom they'd been denied for so long.

Those who knew the criminal questioned how he got away with what he was doing for so long. How nobody caught on, or did anything about the clearly questionable situation the family was in. The Gaffer was known as a drunk, a lazy tyrant, and an all-around bully who spent his days at the pub. It seems nobody figured he spent his nights terrorizing his children.

At one point, The Gaffer's niece had suspicions about her uncle. He visited her dad - his brother - and brought along his two girls. The niece noticed the way her uncle was looking at one of his daughters. "He was staring at her like she was his girlfriend," the woman recalled. She was going to ask him why he was staring so much, but the fear of her uncle got in the way. Plus, she would later say, she couldn't prove it anyway. She knew the hold of control he had over his daughters.

Since 2008, the sisters have been slowly but surely rebuilding their lives from the ground up. They were able to do things they'd never been able to as teens, such as experiment with make-up or buy certain clothing they'd never have been able to wear under their father's tyranny. After so many years of mistreatment and abuse, the sisters finally knew what it meant to live without fear.

The Pockmarked Man

In the chapter "*A Stranger Calls By*" I covered a case that was solved using DNA decades after the crime had been committed. The tale of The Pockmarked Man ends in a similar fashion. But would justice be served this time around?

Between the years 1986 and 1994, the streets of Paris were stalked by a man the press named "The Pockmarked Man" due to his distinct facial scarring. His crimes? Abduction, rape, and murder. His victims? Often children.

The spate of disturbing crimes began on April 7, 1986, when a young girl was making her way to school. She was just leaving the apartment building in which she lived with her family when an unknown figure lurched toward her and dragged her back inside the building. The man certainly had some audacity to attack the girl right outside her home, let alone haul her back in there, dragging her into the basement to carry out his sick assault.

Once confined in the basement with the man, the terrified girl managed to get a good look at his face. She noticed her attacker had a heavily pockmarked face. Presumably, the man didn't care if the child got a good look at his face or not, since his intent was to kill her after he'd carried out depraved acts on her. After the victim had been raped, the heavily scarred man tied a cord around her neck and strangled her to death - or so he thought. Leaving the bloodied young girl on the basement floor, the man absconded from the scene.

He had no idea the girl would make it out of the attack alive, but by some miracle, she had - and managed to tell the police exactly what her attacker looked like. The thing she noticed most was the texture of his skin, and authorities noted this distinguishing feature in her case file.

Still, there were no leads or evidence to help them capture the rapist and would-be murderer. Investigators were sitting ducks, but they had no doubt the man would strike again, although they didn't bank on him offending so soon after his attack on the little girl who survived.

The next attack took place on May 5, less than one month after the previous attack. Yet again, a little girl was the target for the man, and her name was Cécile Bloch. As before, she was making her way to school, leaving her family's apartment, and entering the elevator to head out on her routine school walk. As she entered the elevator, an unknown man stepped in with her, forcing the youngster into the building's basement with him. Again, he assaulted Cécile in the same manner as before, raping the victim before violently lashing out. This time, however, he used a knife to execute his young victim and did so with such force and viciousness that he broke the child's spine. Yet again, he fled the bloody scene, leaving Cécile to be found partially naked in the basement. An unused piece of carpet had been strewn over her small body, but the blood seeped from beneath it. She was 11 years old.

Meanwhile, Cécile's mother was at work, but as usual, called the home phone at lunchtime to make sure her daughter had made it home and had eaten some food. The phone rang with no answer. She tried again, and again. It wasn't like her daughter to not pick up, so Suzanne Bloch called up the school to ask if Cécile was there. She wasn't, she was told, and she hadn't shown up at all that morning. Panic set in. Suzanne rang her husband, and the parents immediately contacted their building's patrolman to ask him to scour the building for their daughter. He did as he was asked, and the little girl was found.

This time, the unknown man who carried out such a despicable crime was spotted at the building before the attack was carried out. The man didn't live in the building and wasn't visiting anyone there. He had no business being there, and as such, witnesses noted the strange man loitering in their complex. Again, they noticed his pockmarks, something the little girl in the first assault mentioned about her attacker. The crime was almost identical, apart from the manner in which the man killed his second victim. It seemed he'd learned his lesson from the first attack, and made violently sure that the next girl he targeted would die. This time, he brought along a knife to make sure.

The French press had caught wind of the attacks and noted the suspect's distinguishing feature by referring to him as "The Pockmarked Man" in their papers.

Sadly, this was the only information the police had. They had no other evidence, no tangible leads, and no anonymous tips coming in. Again, they were sitting ducks. Surely, he'd strike again, but this time, the killer waited almost a year before he did. He switched up his modus operandi this time, too, including his victim selection.

On April 28, 1987, an unimaginable bloodbath was discovered in the affluent neighborhood of Marais, Paris. The Politi family owned an apartment there, which on that particular day was inhabited by Gilles Politi and the family au pair, Irmgard Müller. Irmgard, originally from Germany, had been working for the Politis for some time and was tidying the home that morning when there was a knock at the door. Unknown to Irmgard, pure evil awaited her as she opened the front door.

What truly went on in the apartment that day, and the depths of depravity that Gilles Politi and Irmgard Müller endured, is still unknown. However, the bits we do know about are horrifying. Gilles had been stripped of all his clothing, then was made to lie face down on the ground. The naked man's arms were tied behind his back, as were his feet, rendering him totally incapacitated. While he was laid vulnerable on the floor, unable to see what his attacker was doing or where he would next strike from, Giles was cruelly tortured. The man has cigarette burns all over his body, inflicted by the wicked man who seemingly took joy in the fear he was evoking from his victim.

While this was going on, Irmgard was hanging from one of the family's bed frames. Both her arms were tied together, which were then tied to the top of a bunk bed, also rendering her immobile. She too was tortured via burns, and the killer also tormented her with a knife, too. When he was done, he ended their lives by slashing their throats.

This double-killing seemed personal. Investigators came to the conclusion that the man who did this was romantically involved with Irmgard, considering the way in which the victims were killed and how the au pair had seemingly let the man in the apartment without question. On top of this, witnesses had spotted the man entering the apartment after speaking to Irmgard through the apartment intercom the day prior to the murders, and again on the day of the killings.

However, there were no leads, no evidence, and nothing to guide investigators back to the murderer.

Six months later, The Pockmarked Man resumed his targeting of young girls. His victim would be a 14-year-old making her way home from school. The teen was pulled aside by a police officer who stunned her by explaining he needed to bring her in for questioning. She had no reason to believe the man was not a member of law enforcement; after all, he was dressed like a police officer.

Nervous at perhaps being in trouble, the girl did as the officer asked, but soon found herself in handcuffs in a nearby apartment. Little is known about this crime or the girl, but the attacker raped his young victim as he did in previous assaults. Unlike his first three attacks, he let the girl live. He left her alone in the apartment to deal with the difficult aftermath. She had to pick herself up, tell her parents of her terrifying ordeal, and endure lots of police questioning. Again, the victim had been able to accurately tell police what the man looked like, and it seemed The Pockmarked Man had struck again. Frustratingly, the police yet again had no evidence other than a detailed description of the man.

For years, the attacker kept a low profile. It seemed his attacks had stopped, or perhaps he'd died since there had been no more reports of the man targeting children. Before the parents of Paris could breathe a sigh of relief, The Pockmarked Man turned up yet again. By now, it was 1994, and that summer, a young girl named Ingrid was riding her bike around her quiet neighborhood in Mitry-Mory. The area is surrounded by countryside and is a picturesque commune with a small population. That fateful summer afternoon, 11-year-old Ingrid was cycling beside the railroad tracks, making her own entertainment as she played in the sunshine. As she was minding her own business, a car pulled up beside her. The man was a police officer, he told her, and that she had to get in the car.

The young girl was fearful she was in trouble, so complied with the policeman's demands. After the girl got in, the man drove for over an hour, until he arrived at a place that didn't look like a police station at all. It looked like a rundown old farm. That's exactly what it was, and Ingrid's fear escalated. Initially, she was scared she was in trouble, but now she was fearful for her life. She had no clue who this man really was, nor what he was going to do to her.

The farm, located in the south of France, would be where Ingrid was assaulted for some hours. Her horrifying ordeal ended when the pockmarked figure took off from the scene, leaving a traumatized young girl to summon help.

Police figured The Pockmarked Man had once again secured another young victim. Although they'd gone almost a decade with no arrests - not even any tangible leads - they had been putting pieces of the puzzle together in the background. As more crimes came to light, investigators had been adding more details to the criminal's case file. By the late 80s, the police began to suspect the killer was someone on the inside; that he was one of them. This checked out when The Pockmarked Man began using a police disguise to lure his victims in. Investigators began to realize the man wasn't using a "disguise" at all - they concluded he was carrying out these crimes in his normal workwear.

This theory gained further traction when surviving victims told police how the man who attacked them had a working walkie-talkie - just like the police - and was carrying standard police equipment such as handcuffs. It seemed like the killer was using his knowledge of policing procedures to keep himself off their radar, too. He knew just what to do to avoid capture, and how to avoid leaving any incriminating evidence. Or so he thought: DNA testing wasn't a thing when The Pockmarked Man began his crimes. As the years rolled by, forensic science became a standard way of capturing a killer.

Other little pieces of evidence also pointed to the killer being a policeman. When Gilles and Irmgard were murdered, the location was close to an area where police training was taking place.

Back to DNA testing, it seems a vast number of police forces are now retrospectively investigating older crimes by using the help of science. Cases from the 70s, 80s, and 90s are now being looked at with fresh eyes and the use of DNA testing, where the culprit's DNA was gathered from the crime scene. It seems The Pockmarked Man didn't bank on science evolving as rapidly as it did in his lifetime, so when his semen was recovered from Irmgard Müller, at that point in time, there was still no way to tie him to the crime with that evidence. The same goes for the stubbed-out cigarettes he used to torture his victims; he left them strewn around the murder scene, clearly confident they wouldn't be used as evidence. Now, though, they could be used conclusively to pin the killer to the crimes.

For those who have committed serious crimes like this, it seems they're on borrowed time, as retrospective DNA testing is becoming frequently utilized. It took until 2021 for his past to catch up with The Pockmarked Man, but it eventually did, although perhaps not in the way you'd expect.

Investigator Nathalie Turquey had been tasked with the historic case and took the step of requesting DNA samples from each policeman who was active in the same areas The Pockmarked Man committed his crimes.

François Vérove received his summons in September 2021 and was one of 750 former officers who received the same letter. The other 749 policemen could open that letter and know there was no chance their DNA would be tied to those horrific crime scenes. François Vérove opened his letter and flew into a state of panic. His past had eventually caught up with him.

He took off from his marital home in southern France and rented a place to stay in the sandy, Mediterranean-style beach town of Le-Grau-du-Roi. Upon her return home, Vérove's wife discovered her husband had gone. She waited a short while before calling the police. After all, this was most unusual for her husband, and she was worried something awful had happened to him. She was half right; something truly awful had happened, but it was at her husband's hands decades earlier.

At his beachfront rental property, Vérove presumably wondered about his next move. The jig was up. Instead of handing himself in, The Pockmarked Man offered one last cowardly act by overdosing on antidepressants and booze. Before he did this, he wrote a letter for his wife, all but admitting to being The Pockmarked Man. In the letter, he confessed he'd done terrible things in his youth, blaming his acts on impulses he couldn't control. He added that although he'd done bad things in his life, he'd done nothing since 1997, causing investigators to believe there are unsolved crimes out there that Vérove is guilty of.

After Vérove's body was discovered, DNA testing proved he was indeed The Pockmarked Man. No doubt the team dealing with this case is still working to uncover more victims of François Vérove, and I wouldn't be too surprised to hear of more unsolved crimes finally being cracked and tied to the killer. In particular, the "lull" from the late 80s to 1994 might not have been a lull at all; he simply may have gotten away with these particular crimes.

Let's hope any cold cases tied to The Pockmarked Man can finally be brought to a close thanks to his lack of foresight on the use of crime scene DNA. Although he's not here to face his punishment, his victims and their families deserve that small segment of closure.

The Flat Of Horror

Horror movies and gory films have a history of being blamed for inciting violence. Children, impressionable individuals, and die-hard movie fans are often cited as the perpetrators of film-induced violence. Of course, this is an argument that has many sides, but there are two main camps: one side says suggestible people shouldn't watch such movies, and age ratings are there for a reason. This camp believes writers and moviemakers should be able to create whatever art they want without considering how certain individuals perceive their work. The other side says violence and torture on the big screen directly cause certain viewers to act in ways they otherwise wouldn't if they hadn't seen a particular movie.

Personally, while I do think violence in films can spur some people on to act out violence in real life, I believe those people already harbored violent thoughts and feelings. Never have I watched a violent film and thought about recreating it. In the case of Julia Rawson, her killers were obsessed with horror movies and real-life killers. Nathan Maynard-Ellis and his boyfriend David Leesley carried out a murder so heartless and cruel that the police investigating it were truly disturbed by it. Bearing in mind, these investigators deal with brutal crimes daily, but the case of Julia Rawson was especially sickening for them.

Described as having a child-like persona, 42-year-old Julia Rawson was fun-loving and full of life. A keen artist, she was often seen donning paint-splattered clothing, a sign of a good session with her beloved brushes. Art was something she'd been passionate about since she was young, studying the subject at college in her hometown of Stafford, in the West Midlands of England. It was while at college she would meet her girlfriend, Elaine. The artistic duo would try to make a living from their skills, regularly holding a stall in their market town to sell their work. Life was blissful for the pair. They rented a small flat, spent their days creating together, and their evenings having a pint in the local pub.

Eventually, the pair moved an hour away to Dudley, where they rented a small property to open their first store. As well as their art, they sold homemade items such as candles and incense sticks. The year was 2019, and after a few decades together, it seemed Julia and Elaine had finally built the life they'd been dreaming of: a stable income from their passion and a community full of friends. Then, in May of that year, Julia vanished.

Initially, Elaine didn't contact the police. After all, Julia was a popular figure in the small town they lived in, and it could have been that she bumped into some familiar faces and had a few too many beers, ending the night by crashing at a friend's house. Known as outgoing and eccentric, Julia would befriend anyone. She could go to the pub on her own, and end the night with five new best friends. After a day passed with no sign of her partner, Elaine began to get antsy. It wasn't like Julia to stay out and not get in touch. Another day passed. Elaine was well and truly worried now, and when Julia did eventually come home, she was going to make sure she knew she was in the dog house. By day three, it was looking less likely she'd have the opportunity to scold her girlfriend. Elaine contacted the police and reported her girlfriend missing.

Retracing the missing woman's steps, it was found Julia was last seen in the Bottle and Cork pub on May 11. From here, the police obtained CCTV from the pub to follow Julia's last known whereabouts. The footage showed Julia making the rounds, chatting to everyone, making new friends, and hugging strangers goodbye when they decided it was time to go home. Towards the end of the night, Julia spotted a man sitting alone at the bar and headed over and struck up a conversation.

The CCTV had no sound, but it appeared to show the friendly woman having an animated, drunken conversation with the man. He seemed happy to chat with Julia, and they appeared to have things in common with one another. The CCTV showed the man rolling up his jacket sleeves to show Julia his distinctive collection of tattoos on his arms, and the woman taking an interest in the unique designs. A few hours rolled by, and the pair were still deep in conversation until the last orders were called out just before 1 am.

Not ready to end the night just yet, Julia accepted the man's invitation to go back to his for some more beers. Little did the sociable woman know, the man she'd befriended that night was a depraved, sadistic fiend. He was horror-film obsessed, and not in the way your typical horror fan loves their movies. This man was consumed by the idea of carrying out his own gory horror scene and fixated on the murderers in slasher films. More than this, it seemed he identified with them. His flat was filled with horror paraphernalia, VHS tapes, DVDs, horror movie action figures, doll heads, doll body parts... a whole plethora of creepy items lined his walls.

Of course, trusting Julia could only see the good in people. Even when she walked into his unkempt flat filled with homemade horror masks, and movie killer figurines, with an assortment of weapons on display, she wouldn't have felt any pangs of mistrust toward her new friend. Her childlike trust makes this case feel all the more heartbreaking.

By May 14, two days after Julia was last seen, police put out still images of the CCTV from the pub to see if anyone could identify the man she'd been speaking to. Frustratingly, the footage was skewed by a light shade covering the man's face for most of the film, but investigators hoped someone would recognize the unusual set of tattoos he'd been showing off and help identify the last person Julia was spotted with.

Luckily, the press release from the police garnered enough momentum for the unknown man to be identified. His name was Nathan Maynard-Ellis, and the hunt was on to find him.

The police had no luck catching him at his address, but they quickly caught up with him in the city center streets. They asked him where he was on the night of May 11 into the early hours of May 12. He said he was in bed with his boyfriend, David Leesley. David corroborated Nathan's story since he was standing right next to him when the police took the man to one side in the streets of Dudley. "Do you know a woman by the name of Julia Rawson?" the police asked. Nathan denied knowing her. He was told a person fitting his description was the last person to have been seen with her, and it was all caught on CCTV. Still, Nathan denied it was him on camera. Police then advised him the person in the footage had the same tattoos as Nathan. Still, he denied it, and his boyfriend backed him up. Still, with too much evidence pointing toward Nathan being the last person to speak to Julia, and with him denying the person in the CCTV being him, police arrested him on the spot.

With Nathan Maynard-Ellis being held for questioning for suspected kidnap, investigators took this opportunity to search his flat. As they entered his property, they were taken aback by the smell. They also noticed he had an abundance of horror movie memorabilia, stacks of books about serial killers, and dolls heads placed around the home as if they were ornaments. It was strange indeed. While it was clear the 30-year-old was obsessed with gore and bloody movies, there was something more unhealthy about his horde of horror. He had various weapons among his display, knives, and axes lining his walls alongside VHS tapes of banned movies and other carnage-filled films.

It didn't take long for investigators to notice something peculiar about the carpet in the property. Some of it had been ripped up and replaced. A further look underneath this carpet revealed blood stains on the underlay, which hadn't been replaced.

Meanwhile, back at the police station, Nathan's boyfriend had changed his story. 25-year-old David said that Nathan *may* have gone out the night Julia went missing, but if he did, he certainly had nothing to do with her disappearance. Nothing was adding up with the suspect and his partner, and police weren't getting any valuable information out of them; just denial after denial. All the police could do was use CCTV footage from various businesses and locations around Dudley to follow the pair's movements in the days after Julia's disappearance. From this way of investigating, they hoped to crack the case.

The morning after Julia vanished, Nathan was back at the pub, drinking as if nothing had happened. The couple had an uneventful couple of days, with nothing out of the ordinary happening. Then, on May 16, the pair were captured on camera driving to the local household waste center, disposing of a carpet and an old sofa. Investigators had to hope these items were still laying about in the dumpsters they were thrown in. As officers raced to try and secure the potential evidence, investigators continued to review any CCTV that captured Nathan and David in the days before their arrest. They found some suspicious footage of the pair carrying heavy-looking bin bags to the local canal. Again, officers were dispatched to go locate the possible evidence the two men had disposed of. Inspector Jim Colclough was one of the men working the case and was tasked with going to the canal to retrieve the big bags. It would be a day he'd never, ever forget.

The bags were found, two of them at least. Inside were the remains of Julia Rawson, who'd been chopped up into 12 pieces before being thrown into the plastic bags and flung into a field near the canal. A ickening discovery, there's no doubt about it. Detective Colclough would describe it as "emotionally difficult." Meanwhile, the sofa and carpet Nathan and David had disposed of had been recovered, luckily. The items were drenched in blood. A subsequent forensic analysis of the evidence showed the blood belonged to Julia. The macabre discoveries pointed directly back to the two men who were being questioned at the police station. Despite being presented with all of this overwhelming evidence, neither man would admit what they'd done. Both of them were denying any knowledge of Julia or what had happened to her, protesting their innocence. Despite their attempts to gaslight and lie their way out of justice, there was no way the men could get away with the despicable crime they'd committed.

This meant the police had to piece together what the two men had done to Julia once Nathan had got her back to the flat. Forensics surmised she'd been beaten over the head, which seems to have been the start of the attack. After being subdued by the attack on her skull, only the two men who slaughtered her know what happened. We can only imagine the terror Julia endured at the flat of horrors - the name the local papers gave Nathan's home - but I've no doubt our imaginations don't even begin to comprehend the things Julia went through. Could her killers have cruelly toyed with the woman for hours before murdering her? Did they torment her, did Nathan use his wall of weapons on her? Among his horror movie merchandise were pliers, a drill, a hammer, and other various tools, including a saw. We know he used the saw to dismember Julia after the attack. We'll never know how he used the other implements prior to ending her life.

While Nathan said he was gay, upon his arrest a woman, who was granted anonymity, came forward to tell police about her horrific experiences with him. She was in a relationship with him when she was younger, and told of a controlling, violent, and abusive relationship. Nathan would abuse her sexually, using a weapon to coerce her into things she didn't want to do. He was obsessed with all things horror films and expressed a desire to kill. So much so, his ex-girlfriend would say, that he'd carry a knife with him when he left the house, just in case he found the right victim. It seems he found that victim when Julia Rawson, in all her kindness, went up to Nathan that fateful May night and struck up a conversation.

It took a while to get the accused to trial, and by the time they had Nathan had amended his story. He *did* attack Julia, he finally confessed; but only because she came onto him. Bear in mind, Julia identified as a lesbian and had a partner at home, so these claims should perhaps be taken with a grain of salt. Instead of rejecting the drunk woman, as most gay men would, he decided to go into the kitchen and get a rolling pin to beat her to death with.

The next logical step for Nathan was to dismember Julia's body and wrap it in bin liners. According to him, by this point, voices in his head were telling him to do it.

Again, there was no mention of the acts between the attack and the dismemberment. From things Nathan's ex had said, he'd always wanted to carry out scenes from horror films, so whatever he did to Julia between subduing her and killing her was likely straight out of a slasher movie. From the body parts found, it was discovered Julia's kidney had been taken out, although there was again radio silence from the accused when asked about what they'd done with it.

The trial saw both men admit to concealing a body and perverting the course of justice, but the pair denied murder. Despite the mountain of evidence against them, neither man would admit the truth. On November 9, 2020, they were found guilty of killing Julia Rawson. Nathan Maynard-Ellis was considered the leader, the one who planned the murder, and David Leesley was viewed as being controlled by his boyfriend. Still, David had done his partner's bidding that terrible night and every day since then and would be sentenced harshly for his lack of cooperation with the police.

Nathan Maynard-Ellis got at least 30 years behind bars, while David Leesley got a minimum of 19. Maynard-Ellis also got what was coming to him for the sexual abuse and violence he bestowed upon his ex-girlfriend. By the victim coming forward to the police, he was finally brought to justice for the historical crimes, being found guilty of four counts of rape and one of attempted rape.

Julia Rawson's family was understandably devastated throughout the whole ordeal. But to make the unfathomable situation worse, the trial never got them the answers they wanted. They never got the hows or whys they needed from the trial, since neither man would say anything about the crime they'd committed. *Why choose Julia? What did the men do to her when they had her captive in the flat? Was she aware of what was going on?*

In a statement after the sentencing, Julia's family released a statement. In it, they said they can "only pray that Julia knew nothing about these abhorrent acts." We can only hope that's the case.

Terrible Twins

For those who have twins in their family, or indeed are a twin, they'll know these siblings share a unique bond. Aside from often looking similar, sometimes identical, twins tend to think the same and have the same tendencies, preferences, and instincts. Some say twins have a form of telepathy, and that when one hurts, the other does too. It's a fascinating thing, especially the more you look into it. Stories of one twin feeling a random aching pain in their arm, only to discover their sibling had broken their arm the very same day. Twins who were separated at birth, only to go on and have the same careers, and hobbies - even giving their children the same names, despite never meeting one another. It's something that doctors and scientists don't have an answer for.

That means, then, there's no scientific explanation for twins who kill. *Is it nature? Nurture? A perfect storm of both?* Or some shared telepathy, where one sinister twin passes their dark thoughts to the other, causing both to act in malevolent ways? Killer relatives, although rare, do exist. I covered a case involving killer cousins in *Volume Two*, although, unlike the criminals in that story, the crimes of Robert and Stephen Spahalski weren't carried out together. Separately, they acted out their darkest impulses, each becoming a murderer in their own right.

Little is known about the twins as boys. Their criminal behavior seemingly began in their teens, although there may have been signs prior to this that the twins may be harboring some violent tendencies. Although it's extremely common for murderers to exhibit cruel tendencies as children, we'll never know what the twins were like as young boys since details of their childhood are scarce. We do know that the boys were primarily raised by their mother since their parents got divorced when the twins were 12. They grew into strong, athletic teens who excelled at sports in school, with both boys being gifted at gymnastics.

The pair were well-liked in school and were invited to parties and social gatherings regularly. They weren't the outcast, meek individuals the media often portrays young, soon-to-be killers as. Quite the opposite, in fact. Still, as the duo hit their mid-teens, their anarchic desires took over, and Robert would be the first to find himself in trouble with the law, and he would go on to be the more deadly of the brothers.

At age 16, in the summer of 1971, Robert was arrested for driving a stolen car. He would also get in trouble for starting a fire at his school. Later that year, just before turning 17, Stephen Spahalski carried out a violent murder. Ronald Ripley, the owner of a store in Elmira, New York, was almost 50 years old when Stephen picked up a hammer and bashed him over the head. The teen had struck the man several times, causing him to collapse in a defensive heap. Blood spilled from the man's head as he lay face-first on the floor, eyes staring ahead. Despite the victim possibly already being dead at this point, Stephen took it upon himself to make sure and picked up a knife before furiously attacking Ronald's body.

It was a vicious attack, there was no doubt about it. What could provoke a young boy to feel such venom toward another person? It took a few months for police to catch up with Stephen, who immediately admitted his guilt. After gaining the easy confession, investigators needed to know why the teen carried out the murder. He claimed he was defending himself from Ronald who was trying to take advantage of him sexually. Not taking "No" for an answer, the only way to stop Ronald from making advances toward the young boy was to kill him. That was Stephen's story anyway, and with the victim unable to ever give his side of the story, we'll never know if it was the truth, a half-truth, or a complete lie.

The subsequent trial was quickly over, with Stephen admitting culpability. Since the boy was 17 when he carried out the crime, he avoided life in jail. He was convicted of manslaughter in 1972, not first-degree murder, so an eventual release was on the cards. But, just like his twin, he'd find it hard to avoid a life of criminality.

While Stephen was behind bars, Robert would continue his small-time criminal antics. The law would catch up with him for a robbery he committed where he stole thousands of dollars worth of goods from a music store. It seemed Robert just couldn't keep himself out of trouble, and whatever criminal impulses he had, he'd act upon without a second thought. Authorities hoped a five-year sentence for the theft would quell Roberts's criminal ways, but after serving just two years behind bars, he was released to commit more offenses yet again. In 1976, Robert was back in jail for breaking into a school. He was sent to the same prison where Stephen was serving his manslaughter sentence, and most of the inmates and officers couldn't tell the Spahalski's apart. This could have worked in their favor when one of the twins made a break for it inside an old army truck.

While serving their time at Auburn Correctional Facility in 1978, the brothers were helping service old trucks. One of them made plans with another inmate to hide inside it when the truck was fixed and flee the correctional facility by hitching a ride. The twin and his accomplice never made it out of the prison since officers were tipped off about the escape plan. However, officials now had a new issue to deal with: they had no idea which twin was planning on making a break for it. Robert and Stephen look exactly the same to everyone but their mother, and with neither twin admitting to being the one who was attempting to scape, officials sent both of them to solitary confinement. To this day, nobody knows which twin almost escaped, and they both point the finger at one another.

In late 1979, Robert was released. He had the chance to start fresh, to make something of his life, and to put his criminal past behind him. He was still young and was a capable and talented man. He started off well, getting steady employment as a mechanics helper. A regular paycheck, a roof over his head, a stable environment, and freedom seemingly wasn't enough to keep Robert from reoffending, however. In 1981, just two years after his release, he got in on a plot to steal a coin collection worth thousands of dollars. He was caught, however, and was handed two to five years behind bars.

His release and eventual return to jail seemed inevitable. Up until this point, Robert's crimes had been geared around theft or break-ins. He was yet to explore his violent side. In 1990, that would change. The 35-year-old would commit his first murder.

After his last release, Robert moved to Rochester, New York. It was here he'd become addicted to crack cocaine, and his addiction saw him turn to sex work to feed his habit. Robert would also hustle to make a few bucks, a burglary here and there, but sex work was where the bigger and faster money was. Now Robert had an addiction to feed, he found himself in the regular company of other addicts.

One of them was Moraine Armstrong. The 24-year-old was found dead in her apartment on New Year's Eve, 1990. Her lifeless body was discovered nude, and she was lying with an electrical cord pulled tightly around her neck. There weren't any clues or leads to find a suspect, let alone make an arrest, so Moraine's case went cold for many years. Her good friend, and neighbor, Robert Spahalski knew who did it, and lived with the knowledge for a long time. Even when he was questioned by police, he convinced them he had no idea who would want to murder his young neighbor. All the while, he was well aware he was the one who'd wrapped the cord around Moraine's neck and pulled as hard as she could until she stopped breathing.

It seems this event unearthed Robert's hidden lust for death. Six months would pass before he struck again, this time ending the life of his girlfriend, Adrian Berger. The length of time taken to discover her body, coupled with the thermostat in her home being purposely turned high, meant the body has decomposed rapidly. Adrian was a fellow drug user and sex worker, and this is allegedly how she met Robert. It would be a meeting that proved fatal for the young woman. By cunningly tampering with the heat in Adrian's apartment, Robert managed to escape justice yet again. The body was far too deteriorated to determine a cause of death, although murder was highly suspected. Still, there was no evidence to connect her boyfriend to her death.

It seemed there was no stopping Robert by this point. The next killing came soon after.

In October 1991, Charles Grande, a 40-year-old business owner, was driving carelessly around the streets of Webster, New York. When he was pulled over by police, he charmed them into letting him go, telling them about his landscape business and enamored them with his wit. Little did the police know, the real Charles Grande was lying dead in the bedroom of his home, a horrific catalog of bashes to his skull ending his life. It was Robert Spahalski driving Charles' car, pretending to be the man he'd coldly killed with a hammer.

By the time Charles' body was discovered by his wife, police suspected Robert of being involved in the killing. After bringing the serial criminal in for questioning, it was decided they didn't have enough evidence to secure an arrest for Charles' murder. Instead, though, the police charged Robert with impersonating Charles, something Robert would challenge and later be acquitted of. While the police had no choice but to let the criminal back on the streets, they knew it wouldn't be long before they saw him again. Over the course of the next few years, Robert was predictably in and out of jail.

In 1999, his brother Stephen was released from prison. Stephen had been in jail since he was 17, and almost three decades later, found himself in a brand new world upon his release. Freedom overwhelmed him, and so did his criminal urges it seems. After just six months out of jail, Stephen was back inside after trying to rob a bank in Elmira, New York. It's been theorized that Stephen robbed a bank not for the money, but to get himself a ticket back into jail. His attorney claimed Stephen was institutionalized and couldn't hack the outside world.

While Stephen was back behind bars, Robert kept a low profile. At least, he wasn't captured for any criminal activity. That was until late 2005, but it wouldn't be the police who captured the career criminal - he would hand himself in to Rochester police and admit to murder. This time, it was Vivian Irizarry who'd succumbed to Robert's murderous ways. Vivian was a close friend of Robert, and the pair often took drugs together. He led the police to her apartment to show he was telling the truth. Sure enough, he was.

As Robert explained it, the pair were smoking crack together when suddenly, he began hallucinating. He began to believe his friend was a demon and was compelled to kill her in order to get rid of the spirit that was controlling her body. He took a knife, just like his brother did all those years ago, and stabbed his victim multiple times on her body. Robert then blacked out. When he awoke, Vivian was still alive, albeit convulsing and bleeding profusely. Instead of getting her help, Robert had another idea to put the woman out of her suffering.

He wrapped his hands around her neck and murdered her. Again, he passed out. When Robert came around, he said he felt shame over his actions and took her to the basement and laid her down after bathing the blood off her. Here, he says he spoke to his victim and apologized to her for what he'd done. As the days passed, Robert was unable to shake the guilt over his latest kill. He was close to Vivian, and for some reason, felt the urge to confess about this particular killing.

When he sat down with police to admit to his crime, he also divulged about the other murders, too.

He admitted to killing Moraine Armstrong after the pair had slept together. Afterward, Robert claimed Moraine demanded money. Robert felt like he wasn't a client, he felt they were close. He'd just shared his bag of cocaine with her, too. Her demands for money enraged Robert, so he killed her. He told the police about Adrian Berger. Then there was the Charles Grande killing. According to Robert, he and Charles had a sex-for-money arrangement, and on this occasion, Charles had short-changed Robert.

From the confessions, Robert was charged with the four murders and was given 100 years behind bars for his crimes. As he was sentenced, he apologized to his victims and their families. Robert will die in jail for the series of murders he committed. Stephen, who was also in jail at this point, had no idea his brother was a killer.

"I thought I was the only murderer in the family," he would say upon hearing about his brother's latest sentence.

It's been reported that Stephen is free once again and is back living in his hometown of Elmira, and has kept out of trouble with the law. However, if his attorney was right about Stephen being institutionalized, it may not be too long until the man returns to prison, alongside his brother.

Let's hope the attorney was wrong.

Despicable Dad

A father's role is to support their child's emotional well-being, to offer a source of comfort and security, and to guide their offspring down the right path in life. For John Battaglia, that's just the type of father he was. He was a calm, nurturing parent who never raised his voice to his two little girls, Mary Faith, born in 1992, and Liberty, born in 1995. He doted on them, showering them with love, and words of affection, and was always up for playtime with the happy youngsters.

The same couldn't be said for the way he treated his wife, Mary Jean Pearl, however. John would abuse her emotionally, verbally, and eventually, physically throughout their nine-year marriage. Despite John's maltreatment of his spouse, Mary Jean never dreamed her husband would be capable of ever harming his two daughters. Heartbreakingly, Mary Jean couldn't have been more wrong.

After almost a decade of enduring her husband's cruel treatment, Mary Jean grew so fearful of him that she filed for divorce. She didn't want her little girls growing up to see their mother being mistreated, and for them to think that it was okay to put up with it. Sadly, this would only balloon her soon-to-be ex-husband's vengeful temper.

John Battaglia was born in August 1955, to a family constantly on the move. His father was in the army, and as such, the Battaglia's were never stationed in one place for too long. John, although intelligent, was a restless youngster, and ended up getting involved with drugs as a teenager. His dabble with illegal substances got John in hot water with the law, and to help get himself back on the straight and narrow joined the Marines.

He quickly moved up the ranks, becoming a sergeant, but his heart wasn't truly in it. He'd previously attended university to study accounting, but his dalliance with drugs saw him drop out. John ended up pursuing his dream role of being a businessman and left the Marines to resume his accounting career. He moved to Dallas, Texas, since his dad had settled there, and made money by modeling as a day job while he took accountancy classes in the evening. He eventually became a certified accountant, a successful one at that.

Life seemed picturesque for John. He'd married a woman named Michelle, with whom he had a young daughter. His career was on the up. They had a big house in Dallas with a brand-new car on the spacious driveway. However, inside the quaint home didn't offer the same charm you'd see on the outside. John was abusive to his wife, his short temper often exploding to the point of violence. During one assault on Michelle, John punched her so hard in the face that he broke her nose. She often sported yellow and purple bruises on her face as a result of her husband's anger. Unlike a lot of domestic abusers, John wasn't shy about attacking his wife outside of the marital home. Some of the barbaric assaults took place in full view of witnesses, including at bus stops and other public places. One of those places was even outside the gates of his daughter's school, an attack that was witnessed by many.

In 1987, Michelle was hospitalized after another violent attack from John, and her husband was finally arrested. He pled guilty to a misdemeanor and was given two years on probation. It seemed like Michelle's hellish relationship was over, and she was finally free of the monster in her life. While John had lost his verbal and physical punching bag, it wouldn't be long before he found another.

Mary Jean Pearle would be the man's next victim. Of course, he didn't reveal his true colors straight away; if he did, no one would have ever married him. He charmed and seduced Mary Jean, and the pair married in April 1991. On the wedding night, Mary Jean saw a small glimmer of the man she'd really married. John snapped at his wife, something he'd not done before, and Mary Jean was shocked at the way her new husband spoke to her. She decided to put it to the back of her mind and call it a one-off. It most certainly wouldn't be a one-off. It reminded me of the quote from poet Maya Angelou, "*When someone shows you who they are, believe them the first time.*" However, we try to see the best in people, and cast aside their downfalls as flaws or one-offs, like Mary did. In reality, John was showing his wife exactly who she'd just married.

The first child came shortly after the wedding, and baby number two came in 1995. Even now, Mary Jean would tell you what a brilliant dad John was. He adored his children, and never so much as raised his voice to them, let alone laid a finger on them. Home videos showed the father messing around with his girls, who you could see were just as enamored with him as he was with them. From blowing out birthday cake candles to excited Christmas mornings, the Battaglia family archives show a dad who was extremely involved in his kids' upbringing.

However, John's treatment of Mary Jean was too much for her to handle and she filed for divorce. By 1999 it was on its way to being finalized, and toward the end of the year, it seemed the exes had found an amicable way to co-parent. On Christmas morning of that year, however, John headed to Mary Jean's home to pick up Mary Faith and Liberty for the church service. John wasn't allowed inside the house, and would normally wait outside for his girls to run to the car, but that day he entered the premises. An argument between the former couple ensued, resulting in John following Mary Jean up the stairs as she tried to get away from the altercation. He grabbed his former wife and beat her mercilessly, punching her repeatedly in the back of her head. His two daughters witnessed the attack, terrified for their mother, powerless to stop their father's brutal beatdown.

Paramedics arrived and pleaded with the woman to go to the hospital for a scan. The dangers of being punched in the back of the head are enormous; it can cause irreparable damage to the spinal cord, as well as a number of cognitive issues. Still, Mary Jean refused. It was Christmas Day and she didn't want to ruin it any more than it already had been for her girls. She resumed the holiday like normal, although she was suffering from the throbbing pain of the multiple punches she suffered to her skull. As a result of the attack, John was arrested, charged with assault, and put on probation for yet another attack on one of his partners. John was prohibited from being around Mary Jean for two years and wasn't allowed to see his children for 30 days, but visitation resumed after this period.

The following year, the divorce was finalized, although John was harassing his ex-wife, therefore breaking a stipulation of his probation. He'd leave menacing voicemails for her, being crude and abusive. He'd call her names, swear at her, and throw unfounded accusations her way. One such voicemail was left on one daughter's answerphone, meaning the kids had to listen to their father's tyrannical rants.

Sick of the abuse, Mary Jean called John's probation officer to report his harassment. A warrant for his arrest was put out, and when word got back to John that he was going to be arrested he was concerned that officers would do so in front of his kids. Worried about this happening, John made arrangements to hand himself in without having to be cuffed or suffer any embarrassment. Still, John would call his ex and thank her for calling his probation officer, calling her a "pig." It seems his brush with the law wasn't enough to stop his abusive behavior. To top it off, John had also tested positive for using marijuana while on probation, which was another violation against him. Still, he poured all his anger and blame onto Mary Jean.

Regardless, Mary Jean spoke with John's probation officer and made it clear she didn't want her ex to get in trouble. She wanted him to continue his prosperous business and to have a nice life - she just wanted to get him some help. She stressed that she didn't want her daughter's father to be taken away from them.

John decided he would have one last meal out with his children before handing himself in. Mary Jean dropped the kids off with him in their usual meeting spot - a busy car park - and waved goodbye to her babies. What she didn't know is that someone had tipped John off that Mary Jean had made another call to the police about him after his incessant voicemails showed no sign of relenting. Knowing that this information would only go against him, he was seething toward his former spouse. He didn't let on to Mary Jean that he was incensed at her, although as he drove away from the meeting point that day, Mary Jean remembers him staring at her angrily. She felt uneasy, but again, didn't ever feel like John would do any harm to her children.

That would be the last time she ever saw her babies alive.

Mary Faith and Liberty were looking forward to having a meal with their dad that evening, but he told them he didn't feel too hungry since he was getting arrested because of their mother. He said he lost his appetite because he wasn't going to see his girls for a long time.

Meanwhile, Mary Jean was driving to a friend's house to have a catch-up while her kids were with their dad. When she got there, she received a message saying her girls needed to talk with her because they had a question for her. Mary Jean called John's number and asked what the girls wanted. The angry father put his eldest on the line, Mary Faith. "Hello," the little girl said, to which Mary Jean heard John demand in the background, "Ask her." In response, Mary Jean asked her mother why she wanted daddy to go to jail.

In response, Mary Jean asked her to put John back on the line. "Don't do this to the girls," she pleaded with him, but she didn't get a reply. Instead, all she could hear at the other end was her baby girls begging their father to stop. "Please don't do it, daddy," they cried. Mary Jean was understandably panicked and yelled down the phone for her kids to run away from their dad, to race for the door and get away from him. The pleas and cries from the girls ended with gunshots, then silence. "Merry fucking Christmas," a vengeful John spat down the phone. More gunshots were fired, and Mary Jean feared the worst. She punched 911 into her phone and begged for help.

As police were dispatched to John's apartment, he called his daughter's bedroom phone, where he left a message for them. He told them they were brave, and told them he hoped they were in a better place. He also managed to fit in more insults to their mother, calling her evil and vicious. Before the police could get to John's place, he took off and went to a bar and a local tattoo parlor and got two red roses inked on his arm. The roses, he said, were his daughters. The ones he'd just shot dead in cold blood. It was outside the tattoo studio that police caught up with him in the early hours, and arrested the murderous father. John struggled throughout the arrest and fought with officers, although he ended up with injuries to his face in the scuffle.

The girls, Mary Faith (1992 - 2001) and Liberty (1995 - 2001) were buried with their grandad in North Dallas.

John Battaglia was sentenced to death for murdering his two little girls. In February 2018, he would meet his maker - but not before taunting his ex-wife as he sat in the execution chair."Well hi, Mary Jean," he grinned toward his ex as she sat down to witness his execution.

Still arrogant in his final moments, John told the executor to "go ahead, please." The 62-year-old was then injected with the deadly potion, to which he closed his eyes awaiting his imminent death. He then opened an eye and cocked a smile. "Am I still alive?" he joked. An odd reaction, most definitely. It seems John was intent on being arrogant until the end. Suddenly, he said he could feel the injection working and a chilling grin covered his face as he closed his eyes. Eventually, the grin faded and he began gasping for air. Twenty-two minutes later, he was declared dead.

Mary Jean got up and walked out of the room, having been given a tiny portion of closure from seeing John put to death.

The mother has remarried, but will forever remain heartbroken over the way her babies' lives were cruelly taken away by their narcissistic, vindictive father. Despite Mary Jean truly never believing that John would hurt their kids, despite him easily hurting her on a consistent basis, it seems all the while he was showing who he truly was and nobody could believe it. Not the law enforcement, who were aware of his domestic abuse tendencies, and not his family, who knew of his short temper. Remember, *when someone shows you who they are, believe them the first time.*

More Than He Bargained For

Rarely does a true crime tale have a triumphant ending. While the culprit may have been apprehended and dealt with by law enforcement there's always a victim or victims who endured a horrific ordeal at the hands of the criminal. Sometimes the victim lives, other times they tragically don't make it out of their nightmare. So, even when a murderer or rapist is sent to jail, it's a bittersweet moment; the victim has to live with the aftermath and deal with the trauma of the event on a daily basis. No amount of jail time will offer a victim the chance to be who they were before they were attacked.

The crimes I've covered so far have been unrelenting, so to close *Volume Three* off, I'd like to end with the other side of the coin. A case where the victim turns the tables on their would-be killer and really sticks it to them. After reading about and digesting some of the most despicable crimes committed, I hope the case of Susan Kuhnhausen will show you how, in the face of evil, a fighting spirit (and some good self-defense training) doesn't go amiss.

Fifty-one-year-old Susan Kuhnhausen was an emergency room nurse at Portland Medical Center. On September 6, 2006, after an afternoon at work, she headed to get her hair styled and then returned to the marital home in Southeast Portland. Expecting to be greeted by Mike, her husband of almost two decades, she was instead greeted by a note from him. "Went to the beach," it read, explaining how a lack of sleep lately meant he needed a little getaway. He'd be back at the weekend, he said. Although Mike and Susan were recently separated, he would stop by to take care of the cats when she wouldn't return home until later in the day. It was creeping toward 7 pm, and Susan planned to spend her Wednesday night relaxing and taking care of some household chores.

She walked through the home, opened the mail as she did, and entered the main bedroom. It was dark in there, almost like she hadn't opened the curtains that morning when she woke. *She was sure she did*, she thought, and as she stood pondering about her movements that morning, a man jumped out from the shadows and hit Susan over the head with a claw hammer.

Throughout the years, it seems the training Susan received for her job had stuck with her. Her first aid training, her self-defense training, her evidence-gathering knowledge... it all pulled together that September night to make sure she survived what could have been her last evening on earth. It all stored away safely in her subconscious until she needed it, and boy did she need it that night.

The unknown man, all 5-foot-9 of him, was beating the woman's head, hiding his face beneath the cap he pulled forward. Wisps of hair were pulled through the back of the cap, suggesting the man had a ponytail... Susan was making sure to note all of the things she was observing. A difficult task considering the situation, but a coolness overtook the woman during the attack, and her sense of clarity enabled her to ensure her safety. She made sure to hold her attacker close so his blows had less of a swing on them. The closer he was the less he could injure her, a tip she'd learned from self-defense training.

While preserving herself, Susan realized the attacker wasn't just there to rain a few blows to her head and then leave. He was there to kill her. This thought brought on a surge of adrenaline, from which she managed to overpower the man. Susan was screaming at her attacker, demanding to know who he was and why he was there. The man stayed silent, wrestling with his victim to free his hands and strike her again with the claw hammer. As well as a significant height difference, Susan was also at a disadvantage due to her bad knees. Still, using a burst of strength, she charged at him with enough power to push him over.

"You're strong," he said as he regained his balance and swung again. This time, Susan grabbed his swinging arm, and yanked the hammer from the attacker's grip, again demanding to know why he was there. "Who sent you?" she pleaded, to which her attacker refused to answer.

Susan now had the weapon, and with the man still fighting to get it back, she responded with blow after blow to his head. She can't remember exactly, but she thinks she landed about three or four clean blows to subdue him. It didn't work. The attacker was now angry and managed to prise the hammer off the 5-foot-5 woman he was trying to kill.

All Susan had now was her bare hands. She used them to grip the man's neck, holding on with such force that his face went a purple hue. Scared of blocking her attacker's airways for too long, Susan let go so she didn't kill him. When she did, she decided to make a run for it. Her attacker still hadn't learned his lesson, though, and pursued the woman, chasing her and punching her head until she fell to the floor. She looked up. A silhouette of a man, clutching a hammer with her blood on it, was hovering over her. Susan jolted up, dragged her attacker to the floor, and bit him as hard as she could. Again, it was smart thinking in a truly stressful situation; Susan thought that if the man did end up killing her, at least her teeth marks could possibly tie him to the gruesome murder. As they wrestled on the floor, Susan's face ended up close to her attacker's crotch. She bit him there, too.

For someone being attacked in a horrific manner, Susan was able to maintain quite a bit of clarity through the ordeal. Even while biting the man as they tussled on the floor, she was also turning his pockets inside out to look for some form of ID. The scuffle ended with Susan finding herself in a prime position to grip her left arm around his neck. Her legs locked onto his body. The attacker was going nowhere; Susan's power, fueled by adrenaline, had proven more mighty than her would-be killers. "Who sent you?" she demanded again, multiple times. No answer. She tried to reason with the man, offering to call him an ambulance and cease her hold of him if he just told her why he was there and who sent him. The man refused.

Eventually, Susan realized the attacker had stopped resisting. She used the opportunity to snatch the hammer from him and race to a nearby house for help. Once in the safety of her neighbors, Susan considered the idea that the attacker had been sent by someone incredibly close to her: her husband. She told her neighbors as much, too. The police were quickly called.

As they waited for the police to arrive, Susan thought back to January 1988, when she first spoke to Mike. The pair met from a personal ad in the newspaper, and after a few phone chats, met up in the February of '88. It was love at first sight, although Susan had already caught feelings for Mike through their dozens of phone calls the month prior. Their first date saw them feeding ducks together, and from then on became inseparable. A Reno wedding was quickly organized, with the pair enjoying slot machines on their wedding night.

While Susan was reminiscing about her husband, she remembered the love bubble burst pretty quickly after they got married. They stopped doing things together. Mike didn't want to do much at all. They ended up living separate lives, with Mike happy to go out to work, then return home to chain smoke in front of the TV. Susan was outgoing and liked company, so enjoyed going out with friends to comedy shows and for lunch. This didn't always go down well with Mike, whose personality was the opposite of his wife's. He would monitor her movements, her spending, and what she was up to.

By the time they'd been together for over a decade, intimacy was off the cards, affection was a long-lost memory, and communication had eroded away. While Susan still cared about her husband and wanted only good things for him, she knew she wasn't happy, and he didn't have it in him to make an effort with their relationship. In late 2005, Susan hit a breaking point with Mike and ordered him out of the marital home. After some resistance, he eventually packed some things and headed to his dad's house.

While Susan didn't want to be around Mike at that point, she held back from changing the alarm code or getting the locks changed. She trusted him not to come and hound her, and didn't feel she needed to go to those extremes to keep her estranged husband away. Plus, he took care of the cats from time to time, too.

A knock on the neighbor's door snapped Susan out of her reminiscing about the last 20 years she'd spent with Mike. Police had arrived, and they made their way to Susan's house. The attacker was lying on the floor, where she left him. He was dead. In his back pocket was the ID card Susan had been looking for. His name was Edward Haffey and he was a known criminal. Susan didn't recognize the name, and her husband hadn't mentioned him before. The woman stayed at her neighbor's house that night, and when she returned home the following day, she spotted a backpack that didn't belong to her. A rummage through the backpack revealed some damning evidence that pointed towards Mike being the orchestrator of Susan's (almost) murder.

The bag had a diary inside with an entry titled, "Call Mike" and her husband's new phone number alongside it. The hitman was now directly connected to Mike, although his whereabouts were still unknown.

As for Ed Haffey, police began looking into his background. From what they could see, he was a bit of a drifter who'd recently found a home at a trailer park and worked at Fantasy Adult Video as a cleaner. Coincidentally, Mike also worked there; in fact, it was Mike who hired

Ed. Just as interesting was his criminal past. A decade and a half before he tried to Kill Susan, Ed had arranged the murder of his ex-girlfriend. For this crime, he spent less than 10 years in jail. He was released in 2003 and moved to Portland, where he would meet Mike Kuhnhausen.

Police were able to trace Mike's movements on the day of the attack via his credit card usage. They continued to trace him via his purchases over the following days. One of the establishments he visited was a pawn shop, where he procured a gun. It seemed like Mike knew the police were onto him, and didn't want to face up to reality. Investigators needed to get to Mike before he used the gun on himself, and when they raided his dad's home, they found a suicide note from him. In the handwritten note, he said all he ever wanted was love, but seemed to mess it up every time. A press release was issued to find Mike, hopefully alive.

Seven days after the hitman had tried to end Susan's life, the police caught up with Mike Kuhnhausen and quickly threw some handcuffs on him. He denied any involvement in hiring a hitman, although told officers that he had nothing to live for anymore. His words were a cause for concern for the police, who placed him in psychiatric care. It became clear Mike was in his right mind, albeit full of self-pity, and was subsequently arrested.

When questioning the suspect, police showed Mike all of the evidence stacked against him: the fact he knew the hitman well and the fact that the hitman had noted his diary to call Mike just before trying to kill Susan. Mike's movements after Susan had overpowered the hitman were also highly suspicious. Still, Mike maintained his innocence, insisting he was at the beach the whole time. While he may have been, that didn't erase the abundance of information that showed he'd orchestrated the brutal murder of his wife. Although Mike was refusing to admit the truth, the police wanted to find out why he'd wanted to end his wife's life.

A quick dive into his finances exposed a motive. Mike had recently lost his job at the video store. He was living with his dad and had no funds to get his own place. Mike was recently made aware that Susan had put her brother on her life insurance policy instead of him. Mike needed money, and the only thing he had was the marital home. If Susan was out of the picture, he could sell it and pocket $300,000.

Interview after interview with Mike saw the man deny all involvement. He even denied knowing Ed, despite records clearly showing they worked at the same place. With Mike remaining tight-lipped, investigators spoke to people who knew Ed Haffey to see if they could offer any new evidence. They got in touch with a criminal friend of Ed's who told them something interesting: Ed had asked for his friend's help to burglarize a home. Later, the pair met with a man - Mike Kunnhausen - who offered the criminal money to help Ed kill his wife. The man declined but remembered the face well enough to identify him to the police.

It was another piece of strong evidence against Mike, who suddenly decided to plead guilty at his upcoming trial. *Not because he was guilty,* he'd stress, but to avoid a longer sentence.

Susan had a lot of things to deal with; not only had she killed a man in self-defense, she had done so because her husband had paid him to harm her. There wasn't just one horrifying aspect of the crime to deal with, but many. She was almost killed. Her husband wanted her killed. She'd taken a man's life because of this; it was all too much to comprehend. And still, her husband was denying it all.

It only took Susan a day after Mike's arrest to file for divorce. The woman had plenty of friends to support her, but her trust in people had totally eroded. The once-vivacious nurse now second-guessed people's intent and found herself becoming paranoid. So much so, she felt like people were following her, and began driving various routes home to avoid being stalked. She spent a lot of time at the shooting range, preparing for the next time a dangerous man broke in and tried to kill her. As she awaited her ex's sentencing, she quipped that she was already doing a life sentence for "picking a bad husband."

While Susan got a life sentence, Mike got seven years for hiring the hitman. It seems like a paltry sentence for such a horrific plot, but Mike would never make it to the end of his sentence. Cancer caught up with him just three months before he was due to be released.

In the aftermath, Susan would speak out about the ordeal, and how it affected her. Many people wanted to know what enabled her to survive the assault and how she overpowered a man brandishing a weapon. She had no choice but to fight back, she said. She couldn't run and she couldn't hide. "You have to fight," she would say of coming face to face with someone wanting to kill her. "You don't know that you won't survive."

Susan is considered a hero for her actions that day, and although she doesn't feel heroic, she showed others, particularly women, that you can face evil and be triumphant. Despite a man losing his life, Susan feels no guilt about the outcome of the awful situation. It was him or her that day, and she chose her own life. A decision we should all make if we're ever faced with evil.

Final Thoughts

We have been confronted with some truly shocking and gruesome crimes throughout these eleven chapters. From serial killers to kidnappers to con artists to sexual deviants, each chapter has shone a light into the darkest corners of the human psyche.

Despite the horrors that these tragic crimes represent, I like to think that we can take some kind of solace in the fact that justice was ultimately served for many of the victims. We can argue that the punishment will never fit the crime, but with the combined efforts of the brave witnesses and survivors, as well as law enforcement, many of the perpetrators in this book were made to answer for their despicable actions. A barbaric criminal behind bars is a win in my book. The alternative - that they're free to walk among us - is an overwhelmingly anger-inducing thought.

I often toy with the idea of what I think adequate punishment would be. I watched a short film not too long ago where a killer's punishment was chosen by the victim's family.

It was set in a world where this was the norm: those affected by violent crimes chose the penalty. The criminal in question had his arm amputated at the family's request. When this didn't change the killer's brash and uncaring attitude, the family then requested his legs be removed. This affected the criminal massively. While this was just an imagined scenario for a film, I'm sure some people would agree that punishment like this should exist. But then, we jump into the issue of morality. There's a fine line between punishment and being inhumane, it seems, even when the punishment is for those who have no consideration for humanity.

A friend of mine also suggested replacing animal testing in favor of "convicted criminal testing." The violent rapists and killers of the world, she argued, should be the ones to endure this, not innocent caged animals. Even those who favor this suggestion may then offer the counter-argument: what if one of those criminals later turns out to be innocent?

True crime is such a complex and frustrating topic, but an important one to discuss, I feel. Opinions and beliefs as to how killers ought to be treated causes a huge divide among followers of the genre. I'd be keen to know your thoughts on justice and what it means for you.

As we close this installment of *Unbelievable Crimes*, I'll repeat my constant reminder of how evil often lurks around the corner. To be forewarned is to be forearmed, as the saying goes. Not just for yourself, but for other people, too; for the vulnerable around us who can't necessarily protect themselves from the predators of the world.

The criminals in this book were once members of our society. They walked the same streets as us. Anybody can be a victim and violent criminals aren't reserved for horror movies or "other people." Stay vigilant, be curious, and as my dad used to tell me, *always expect the unexpected*.

Thank you for taking the time to read this third installment of the series. If you've read through volumes one and two, thank you for your continued support. Words cannot express my gratitude but know that I truly appreciate your readership. Depending on when you're reading this, *Unbelievable Crimes Volume Four* shouldn't be too far from release. If you're reading this after summer of 2023, then it's already released. I hope to see you there, and if you'd like, you can join my upcoming newsletter below. My aim is to have this up and running by the end of this year (2023) and roll out a weekly email of crime stories.

Danielaairlie.carrd.co

Thank you for your support,

Daniela Airlie

Printed in Great Britain
by Amazon

26803373R00066